THE ART

OF A
HUSTLER

PACHINO WILLIAMS

The Art Of The Hustler

By Pachino Williams

Cover Painted by Jillian Williams

Created by Jazzy Kitty Publications

Logo Designs by Andre M. Saunders/Leroy Grayson

Editor: Anelda L. Attaway

© 2022 Pachino Williams

ISBN 978-1-954425-43-9

Library of Congress Control Number: 2022901874

ACKNOWLEDGMENTS

I want to thank my father, Bobby Williams, my mother, Aldreana Williams, my brothers Shannon Williams, Brodrick Williams and my little sister Qubia Williams. My nephews, Daishawn Williams and Shannon Williams Jr. My Niece Makenzie.

I want to give special thanks to my children Samaria, Emani, Jahhlive, and Kayla for being so understanding and loving as I grew as a father and as a man.

To the women God chose to bear my children and the ones I dated. Thank you, and no matter our differences, you all ultimately played a major part in my growth as a man.

To all my friends, associates, business partners, OG's, the junkies I served, the strippers I helped, and drug connections. Everybody that has ever given me good advice, hell even bad advice, because I sill learned from it all. R.I.P. Cory, P-Roe, (P.R) Jonny, Troup, Lil' Dove Dezzy.

I want to thank Tupac, Malcolm X, Martin Luther King, Marcus Garvey, Assata Shakur, and every Black male and female that came before me that made a difference. Thank you for sparking the light that I would use to start my fire.

Thank you to all the authors and great people in history that I quoted in this book. Thank you for helping me go through my struggles by sharing their thoughts and struggles.

Last but not least, I want to thank Allah (God) for giving me the strength, wisdom, patience, intellect, faith, and drive to make it through this life to write this book!

DEDICATIONS

This book is dedicated to Sadie Williams, Loyd Williams, Elizabeth Griffin, Dollie B. Anderson, and Gloria Atkins.

To the Williams, Anderson, and Griffin family.

For my Uncle Ben, Uncle Isaac Williams, Aunt Charlotte, and Aunt Victorene (Thank you for all the conversations) Long live Trey

Lafamila 4 life!

The greatest three quotes I ever heard on this planet were:

"WITH AGE COMES WISDOM"

"KNOWLEDGE IS POWER"

"TIME IS MONEY"

TABLE OF CONTENTS

TABLE OF CONTENTS

INTRODUCTION

This book will inspire and educate everybody in the world; the everyday working man, the corporate lawyer, and the college kid struggling to maintain life. The prisoner without the vision and hunger to succeed. I hope this book inspires the neighborhood drug dealer, robber, conman and serves as a road map that helps them all find their path away from a life of crime.

This book will take you on a journey throughout my life as I evaluate my rights, wrongs, highs, and lows. The first rule to becoming a hustler is to respect the game of life. That respect will aid you to be aware of wolves in sheep's clothing, the villains, the pitfalls, the backstabber's etc. Truth be told, that's all there is in the street game.

Ultimately, I pray that it inspires you to do better in life, to be more than a hustler, a stripper etc. Let's take a second and symbolically say that by reading this book, that small act of aspiration will be the seed that grows into reality. Understanding that growth is inevitable with gaining knowledge which symbolically is your light. Your ambition and dedication are water, and with hard work and time, that seed will grow to a tree, and that tree one day will bear fruit. Symbolically the fruit is your success. That fruit (success) will feed your bloodline for generations.

Readers, did you know that comparatively speaking, when asking people about what they want in life, 95% of the current population can be compared to a ship without a rudder or paddle. Most of us don't know where we are going and are just riding the waves of life. Having no direction whatsoever, yet life's troubles are more than just a wave; there will be storms. I once was just like that 95% just riding the wave, yet through storms, fire, and major life changes. I found my compass my (purpose) to guide my boat in a better direction and destiny in life. I want you to ask yourself this question before the book starts what is your compass?

"There are no mistakes in life, only lessons to learn after you overcome the issue." **Warren Buffet**

DECEMBER 21, 1979

"Imagination is everything; it's the preview of lives coming attractions." **Albert Einstein**

The Mayans predicted that the world would end on December 21, 2000. Oddly, December 21, 1979, that's the day mines started. I always felt that my life started long before 1979 but let me tell you how it started.

My mother Aldrena came from South Florida to Georgia when she was in high school. She was light-skinned, had a beautiful complexion, bright eyes, and pigtailed Indian-looking hair. She always had a flair for fashion and a love for reading, education, and helping people. Most people who meet her say she should have been a schoolteacher or a youth mentor for kids. They never understood that it's just in her nature to be helpful and a good person. Like everyone else in this world, she would find her calling later in life.

Let's go back a little. My mother's mother, Elizabeth Anderson, had eight children, two from my grandfather Mr. Frank Bostick. After his untimely death, she would later remarry and have six kids, which caused issues with her current husband about his stepchildren. This meant that my mother and her sister, my Aunt Sandra, would soon leave for Georgia and live with my great-grandmother, Ms. Dolli B. Anderson. My great-grandmother was a wise old Geechee, Christian woman. When I was a child, she filled my ears with stories of slavery, voodoo, and the struggles of Black people in her lifetime. You see, that's the crazy thing about the time you can't go back. I would give my all to sit and talk with her now because my mentality is different. She gave me jewels that I was far too young to understand. She told me how hard it really was.

My mother's father, Mr. Frank Bostick, was ex-military; he had fought in the Korean war. He was an entrepreneur, some legal and some illegal. He moved around from Georgia, North Carolina, and New York. In New York, some underworld dealings with the Italian mafia left him shot in the head in the front seat of his car. This large extended family would ultimately play a role in my rise to power.

My father Bobby was from South Georgia; his father, Mr. Loyd Williams, was a sharecropper and a God-fearing man; he would eventually own his own business with time, motivation, inspiration, and hard work. My grandfather always was an inspiration in my life because he had to become a hustler. Before I go further, let me explain a hustler is more than a drug dealer or street person. He was my inspiration because he couldn't read well but could count money with his eyes closed. Still, he raised eight children and did an amazing job. For that, he will forever be in my prayers and heart. A devoted Christian and family man, he sat on the Deacon board of his church for decades. My grandmother Ms. Sadie Williams and grandfather were both loving people, yet gangsters as card sharks if provoked or their families well-being threatened. My grandfather told me the story of when he met my grandmother; he said that when he first met her, she was fighting some girl in a ditch. LOL

My grandmother Ms. Sadie Williams was the real deal, no cut. Still, she was a church-going woman who was the most loveable person when needed. She always gave me advice about life, love, fighting, and dealing with the world. Together they had nine children, my father being the second to the youngest. My grandfather provided for his family by any means necessary. He installed that same hard-working mentality in all of my aunts and uncles. That mentality had to be in the DNA because it trickled down to their kids. Therefore, all my cousins had entrepreneurial spirits and a hell of a grind. We were taught to work hard, and then we will obtain what we want in life. My grandmother once told me, "Boy, you have a deep fire in your mind for success, and the only way to put it out is to one day make it."

My parents met in high school and would forever be sealed together, just like penguins they mated for life. My father was a stand-out high school star athlete in football, basketball, and baseball. His name rests on many records to this day. Therefore, he was the big dog on campus. My mother was a feisty but shy fashionista from Florida with dreams of becoming a fashion designer. She was loving, loyal, and had an outgoing spirit, which would create a lifelong bond with her and my father.

I remember my father once told me the first time he saw her; he was awestruck. When he first spoke to her, she was so shy she ran off giggling. They soon would fall in love. My father would later get a college football scholarship and leave for college. At this time, my mother was pregnant with my older brother Shannon in Georgia. My father said he longed for his lady and son dearly. He would drastically hurt his knee and return to Georgia. Blessed with my grandfather's ambition, he would later leave again, going to New York, still trying to find his path in life. While there, he told me he longed for Georgia's red clay and pine trees.

Most importantly, he missed his new family. He soon would return and with my grandfather's drive, respect, and love for his family. When he returned to his family, they got married in 1976. My oldest brother Shannon was three years old.

They moved to Atlanta in 1978, it was rough, but my father is a strong man. He bossed up. My father has always been street smart, book smart, and business-minded. Before he had my older brother, He and his brother built and ran a club out of my grandmother's property which made so much money that my Aunt Maryland, the youngest of his sibling, said she used to steal so much money, and they never knew it. The club was my father's first investment, which turned out great. Later, he would be a club and radio DJ, government employee, real estate investor, and small business owner. Simply put, he had my grandfather's hustle.

On December 21, 1979, I was born; that's also the first day of winter. I've always believed that's why I am so cold-hearted in certain situations. My mother once told me that she was so sick with me during her pregnancy that she couldn't keep any food on her stomach. She said she knew I would be a very selective and picky person; today, I still am. The story goes, my brother, Shannon, asked for a brother and when I was conceived, he then wanted me as a Christmas present. To his disappointment, I came a little early. My mother wanted to name me Frank, after her father, or Michel, after the great archangel. Again, my father declined. She said she was reading a newspaper and saw an advertisement for a movie starring Al Pachino. That was it! Pachino was born. Since that day, my parents have been through so many storms in their lives. Still, they stayed loyal, loving, and dedicated to each other. I often feel that is where I get my perception and dedication in a relationship, yet that's another chapter.

My little Brother Broderick and my little sister Qubia didn't come until later by different circumstances. With their arrival, my mother and father showed me compassion, love, and a duty to humanity. They are my family, and I would go to the end of the world about both of them, their blood no less.

First, my parents never wanted me to sell drugs or be in the streets, period. What parent would want that life for their child? Still, all the bullshit I've been thru, they never let me down. That was the path that I chose and if I had to do it over, I would do it differently. Sure, I had millions of dollars and a life most could only dream of, but at what cost? I lost the best years of my life, my kids' lives. I've lost loved ones to death. Friends, family that I will never talk to or see again. I've lost all sorts of money, houses, cars, etc. Some would say and agree that it's just a part of the game!

I saw the game from the skybox, and I realized that the way I was living was some bullshit. I had piles of money, cars, women, jewels, etc. Still the most beloved person in my world, my mother wouldn't touch a dime of my money. I remember one time when I wanted to take her shopping. My ex-girlfriend wanted to buy her a $100 dress, and she flat out refused. That made me feel horrible and small. Here I was, a drug boss with money to burn, and ironically, the person I love the most sincerely wouldn't spend a penny of it. That day I learned the true meaning of unconditional love.

When I went to prison, she was the only female that never strayed from my side. Well, her and my daughters. My mother would give her last to see me survive. I've dealt with the worst of the worst in the criminal underworld in Atlanta and other major cities. Definitely in the prison system all over Georgia, I've met real killers, robbers, conmen, and drug dealers. I've always remained solid. I never broke the first code of the streets and the dope game. Never snitch! I lost my life to the street code and I am currently fighting like hell to get it back.

I hope this book is a guide to some and a deterrent to others. I don't want people to think that I am glorifying the street life, yet I am simply telling my story. I hope that it shines some light on the street life pitfalls. I hope the people that read this book will pull the next youths' blinders off their eyes and let them see the game for that. It is simply a game. I hope a big homie or an O.G will pull their coattails and tell them. Let's do this a better way. Let's get a business with this money or just find a better way to eat other than selling drugs, prostitution, or robbery. I tell my story not for the street accolades because I have been there already. I got those stripes, hood credit or whatever. I don't need to justify my thug or my masculinity that way. I tell my story so you, the reader or the teacher can make their story better. I hope through reading this, the little kid in the hood simply can find a better way out.

FOOTPRINTS IN THE SAND

One night I dreamed a dream. I was walking along the beach with my Lord. Across the dark sky flashed scenes from my life. I noticed two sets of footprints in the sand for each scene, one belonging to me and one to my Lord.

When the last scene of my life shot before me, I looked back at the footprints in the sand. There was only one set of footprints. I realized that this was at the lowest and saddest times of my life. This always bothered me and I questioned the Lord about my dilemma.

"Lord, You told me when I decided to follow You, You would walk and talk with me all the way. But I'm aware that there is only one set of footprints during the most troublesome times of my life. I just don't understand why You'd leave me when I need You most."

He whispered, "My precious child, I love you and will never leave you, never, ever, during your trials and tests. When you saw only one set of footprints, it was then that I carried you."

Samaria	Emani	Jahhlive	Kayla
3-10-2004	06-01-2005	03-09-2009	06-27-2009

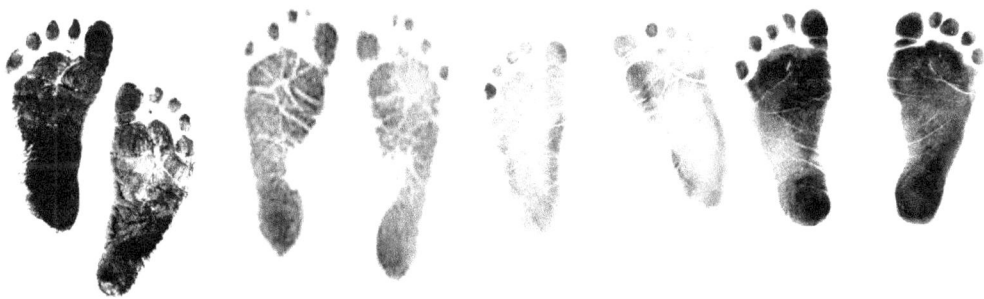

PART I

MONEY, POWER, RESPECT

"A party gives laughter, wine gives happiness, and money gives everything." **King Solomon** (Ecclesiastic 10:19)

GAME - Hypothetically speaking, let's say you are in the narcotics (drug) game, and in the drug game, if your connection is playing games, being greedy. Holding up your money and you want to rob him on the low. The first law on loyalty states that robbery is fair game. My stance is this if you do bite the hand that feeds you. This rule applies to the corporate world and the streets. You have to make sure you have another more eager and willing hand to feed you. Never cut off your own wrist, simply put. (playing yourself short!)

REVERSE - Let's say now hypothetically, you have been head of sales at this company for 10 years, and they won't give you a raise or a better position. Quit, or threaten to quit to check your real value. Similar scenario again hypothetically speaking. If you have been selling drugs for 10 years, and you don't have personally or have touched a million dollars. Quit! You're in the wrong game! Rule # 2 The game starts with a warning that says, "The streets ain't for everybody; that's why they make sidewalks!"

CHAPTER 1

WHEN THEY STOP TALKIN'

"You have chosen war; what will happen will happen and what is to be, we know not. Only God knows the outcome of events." **Genghis Khan**

<u>GAME</u> - Most people on this planet, without knowing it, believe in predestination. Predestination is the thought that everything is written. So, with trials and the storms in life, the majority of people will tell you, "Just be patient, It will get better. What they don't say is, "If it doesn't get better, it will get worse." My advice is never to let someone tell you exactly what to do when dealing with your life. Make all of your own decisions alone, simply because you have to deal with the results alone, good or bad still alone.

<u>REVERSE</u> - With predestination, every situation in your life is already planned. That presumption is spoken in every religion, faith structure or cult. What will happen will happen. So be patient and make sound judgments. If the stars are aligned, you will be the NBA star, NFL star, or the boss of the city you live in. The president of the company or vice versa. Only God knows. My advice is to go hard; no matter what someone else opinion is, it's all invalid but helpful. The best advice is to never decide based totally on someone else's advice. Make your own decision; just use others' opinions, good or bad, for judgment based on your goals.

STORY - I remember when I was around 10, my family moved from Lakewood in Atlanta, Georgia, to Thomasville, Georgia, down south. This strictly parental decision left me and my older brother Shannon devastated. He felt like his life had stopped altogether. The reason being he was five years older, and he was established. Meaning he had good friends and a girlfriend. The move hurt him a lot worse than me.

On the other hand, I would just miss my two friends and a couple of people at school. My brother cried for most of the move; hell, I cried because he was crying. I didn't have the same emotional attachments that he had to Atlanta back then. Still, I kept the city boy swagger and attitude during the transition. Later on, after the crying and frustration stopped. We finally accepted our fate and carried on.

It was a month or so later, the first day of school in Thomasville was quickly approaching, and my brother for days had been mumbling about how lame Thomasville was and how much he hated it. I was sad yet willing and ready for the change. My mom told me it would be different but kool. I knew it wouldn't be like Tullwater Elementary in Lakewood, a ghetto, suburban fashion show. Don't get me wrong, Tullwater was hella fun, but now I was in new territory. Before this week, my father and mother went to downtown Atlanta and did their usual shopping for my school clothes. Armed with my brothers and my requests. They bought all the latest and flyest fashions in Atlanta. Well, the ones the kids were wearing, at least. I figured everything would be kool, and I would be fly to boot.

Weeks later, it was the first day of school. I went inside the school that morning confident like I always did in Tullwater, but now I was in the country with my still growing swagger. I didn't notice the attention I caused. I sat down at the breakfast table feeling like a million bucks. There felt like a million eyes were watching me too. I could feel the curiosity, envy, and jealousy in the air. Unknown to me, it was the first time I was fish bowled (watched like a fish in a bowl). It would be far from the last.

Finally, the first bell rang and with help from a couple of students, I finally found my class. I quickly scanned the room. Then I took a seat next to this mixed girl and a brown skin girl.

The brown-skinned girl asked with a southern accent and a sassy voice, "What's your name?"

I replied with a confident smile, "Pachino."

She giggled, "My name is Latoya and Pa-no-cio is a funny name. you don't look or dress like you are from around here."

I smiled, "I am from Atlanta." We ended up talking most of the period.

Then the teacher called recess, and we all went outside. While standing outside alone, just watching the other kids. I slyly peep a young cat named Jerome with his little crew watching and jocking a young player's moves. Now mind you, I haven't said one word to any males. I just talked to Latoya and a couple of other girls. Latoya and her friends walk over, and they start a conversation. We were all laughing and they asked questions about Atlanta and my old school. I laughed and joked, yet I kept my eyes on the haters using my growing street smarts. I saw that Jerome was the usual alfa male in the area. Just by watching all the young boys following him around.

After about 10 minutes of recess, everyone walked upfront. I was posted on the wall talking to Latoya and four of her friends. Just laughing and joking about my city slang and their country words. I felt like I was having a great first day.

Ever since I could walk, I've always been comfortable around females versus males. My mother said she knew I would give women hell because, as a baby, I was a big flirt. I guess it was just in my blood to love the ladies. My pops, grandpa, mother, father, and Mr. Frank Bostick were all suave playas. Not to get off track, let's go back to the story.

Jerome now walks over with his cronies and post on the wall alongside the females and me. They didn't say anything; they just stood there while the females talked.

After a couple of minutes, he asked, looking in my direction, "What kind of shoes are those?"

Everyone looked at me, then my feet. I was totally caught off guard. Hell, I even looked at my own feet.

Regaining my thoughts, I smartly replied, "Diadora's," I said it in a slick way as if to say he should know what kind of shoe it was.

To my surprise, he laughed and said, "I ain't never heard of their shoes and they ugly as hell!"

I was shocked at first, then replied, "Well, in the city, everyone is rocking these." All the boys laughed, then one of them stepped out from the group sticking his shoes out.

"Well, in the country, we were these."

My brain quickly told my eyes to check everyone's feet. Jerome had on some white Cortez Nikes. That same shoe I had two years ago in Atlanta. They all had them on in different colors. They made a couple of jokes on my shoes, and I just laughed it off and said some jokes back. As we called it in Lakewood, I was used to joneing (telling jokes on people). Now I had everyone laughing. That day I still felt played on the inside and a little cheap, yet I smiled. I knew my shoes were expensive, and I was also fly as hell. I still felt out of place; my great day was now ruined in my eyes. I've always felt self-conscious about my clothes, like my mom said when I was in her womb. Picky! That day I felt myself consciously and constantly checking my feet. That day I didn't feel physical fear, but social fear.

Later on, when I got home. I looked for my dad to confide in him about my day. My grandmother, Ms. Sadie, was there; she told me my father and mother had left and would be back soon. She looked at me in my eyes and could quickly tell something was wrong. she then calmly asked about my day. I sat down and told her about the situation. I felt better just telling her and her being concerned.

After I finished, she smiled and said, "Baby, people will talk about you when you are doing good or when you are doing bad. Dressing kool, or just doing your own thing, but Chino, when they stop talking about you, that's when you have had a bad day, Baby. Why because you probably will be in the grave." I didn't understand it back then, but it stayed in my head throughout my life.

Later on, that day, when my dad got home. I told him about the situation and moped around the rest of the night. I went to school the next morning wanting to hide my feet under the desk all day, which hurt my pride more than my ego. When I arrived home that afternoon, my pops had three new pairs of Nike Cortez on my bed, to my surprise. In three colors blue, red and black. I jumped up and down with joy. I realized when I was older that the Diadora's were $100 and the Cortez was like $40. My father was probably happy as hell because they were hella cheaper. I still was ecstatic. I wore a new shoe every week for the rest of the month. The kids now looked at me differently, like I was kool. They never understood I just wanted to be fly like my pops. My mom laughed like hell one afternoon when I came home about the situation.

She said, "Chino, I don't understand you, son you beg for $100 shoes. Now you leave them home and wear $40 shoes. Baby, I don't understand you or those crazy kids."

GAME - As I got older, I realized that I should've taken my grandmother Sadie's advice a lot younger and kept rocking my own style. Real players, movers, shakers, and bosses for one special reason. In whatever game they play, whether it's basketball, drugs, pimping, or whatever. They change the game and don't play it like the lames. I was destined to be a coach instead of a player.

(1) "There is no such thing as bad publicity except your own obituary." Remember, these people would talk about you if you got Bally's on your feet or Pro Kids. If you are rocking Levi's on your ass or Louis Vuitton. You have to learn early in life that you can't please everybody. Mastering this skill like any other skill is detrimental; the trick is to learn this lesson as soon as possible. That way, you can spend less time worrying about your peer's opinions and more time focusing on getting your own life straight. You have to mentally do you, regardless. Get your money, education and do whatever makes you feel happy.

(2) "Never change for the mainstream, stay in your own lane and if you're talented and resilient enough, the mainstream will come to you." If

you want to be a singer, poet, or whatever, do you. Suppose you want to open a business selling TVs, hats, or remote-control cars. Whatever it may be, you have to do what makes you feel good. Simply because rich, poor, flashy, or ashy people are going to hate, so you are better off being yourself and finding your own happiness. Everybody on this planet we call earth is incomparable. Everyone shows their uniqueness through their music, clothes, cars etc.

(3) Understand you are one of a kind; your character traits are a kind of chemical mix that will never be repeated in history. There are ideas unique to only you. You hold a specific rhythm and perspective that are your strengths, not your weakness. You might not be afraid of your uniqueness and careless of what people think of you. There's an old saying that states, "You damned if you do or damned if you don't." You might as well do what helps your progress in life. Remember, people will always judge you no matter what. As you gain power, popularity, or fame, the people around you will feel envious, this is inevitable. Some will show it and some will not, but the inevitable will happen; people are going to hate. If you think poor, you are poor.

(4) "Your only real fear should be that you will start to listen to what other people say about you one day." I once told my ex-girlfriend Simone that her friends didn't mean her any good. Like most people, she got upset.

Then she said, "You don't even know them. How could I judge them?"

I explained that it was fairly easy. Every time I was with her and they saw us, they only spoke about her new clothes, shoes, jewelry, or whatever she had on. It was odd because they would do this before even saying hello. She thought I was crazy or just overprotective. She didn't see their envy or jealousy in their words or looks.

(5) "We think that what matters in the world is gaining attention and making friends. These misconceptions and naive are brutally exposed in the light of the real world." Later on, those same friends would introduce her to another guy, and one even stole from her. Simply trying to hurt her and me. They didn't want to see her happy and with the person providing those same nice things for her. She couldn't read in between the lines. I, on the other hand, was expecting their crosses. When I found out about her infidelity, I left her. To be honest, that decision hurt, but ultimately I couldn't trust her anymore. The friends were happy now that she was lonely, struggling, and living with her mother. Years later, she would tell me that she had made a mistake and wanted me back. It was way too late; the damage was done.

(6) "For it is a great rule of human nature that people despise those who treat them well and look up to those who make a concession." We all have had people compliment on our new things, which is normal but beware of the excessiveness. They mean you no good, read between the lines of these compliments their praise, their slick remarks. Judas kissed Jesus before he backstabbed him. Caesar was killed by his friends. Watch for the signs; watch for the envy in their eyes. The sarcasm in their voices. Some will hide it very well; others can't hide it. The hate oozes out of them in her eyes, their voice, and body language. They don't even realize it, and they don't know that they just showed you they are throwing salt. (shade, or hating)

(7) "It takes courage to grow up and turn out to be who you really are." In street terms, the definition of a hater is a person that cannot congratulate

another person for an accomplishment or doing something they are not doing or cannot do. They are easy to spot, but the most dangerous of haters is an envious friend. They will hate silently for years, even losing sleep. Disgusted about your accomplishments in life. These people which whom you are intimately involved with never reveal the hate. Still silently preying you to fail in life yet smiling in your face the whole time. You have to learn for yourself and to do that, you have to be comfortable being you. Never conform to the public's wishes or perception of who you are.

(8) "As an egotist of the strong variety, you trumpet your own horn, indicial and take a great pride in your accomplishments if others cannot accept that, or judge you as arrogant that is their problem, not yours."

God does not judge man until the end of days, so why should you or I? Learn to use your instincts. Your mind will tell you a lot of times when things are wrong or right. Learn to watch people and never let them know that you are aware of their envy if you have co-workers or business partners, even people around you who try to change you for the worst. Then you must reverse it and change your friends. Find people who love you and respect you for who you are. Never conform to their wishes because you have to be happy before making others happy.

(9) "A weak person goes where he is smiled at." If you are broke, people will talk; if you are rich, they will still talk. If you are uptight or have a free spirit, people will talk. The public will always have a perception of who you should be. The deepest principle in human nature is the craving to be accepted. This desire is what lures many boys into becoming gangsters. Conforming to people's wants leads to many problems, depression, isolation, or even worse, a situation that could get

you in trouble or, even worse, killed.

As humans, I think we must all remember this great quote.

(10) "I am the owner of my might and I am so when I know myself as unique." Beware even when you expose who you really are. Everyone will react differently; some will flee away from you and some will flock toward you and love you more. So why not just be yourself and attract the people who love you for you, no matter what you do in life. No matter what you do, you will have envious people. There is a hater for every person on this planet. What is even crazier is the fact that you are someone hater also.

(11) "If you are dependent on their judgment for your sense of worth, then your ego will always be weak and fragile. You will have no center or sense of balance. You will wilt under the circumstances and soar too high with any praise. Their opinions arc merely helping you shade your worth, not your self-image. If you make mistakes, if the public judges you negatively, you have an unshakable inner core that cannot accept such judgment, but you remain convinced of your own worth." Too much praise makes you weak! The reason I chose this topic for the first chapter is simple. You have to know yourself and build a strong foundation of self-worth before building an empire. Let them talk!

(12) "If you have no self-confidence, you are twice defeated in the race of life, with confidence you have already won, even before you have started." Refuse to conform, refuse to be stamped! Do your own thing.

CHAPTER 2

HOMEWORK WIN'S THE GAME

"The law that governs circumstances are abolished by new circumstances." **Napoleon Bonaparte**

GAME - Granted, nothing in life will remain the same. There is an old saying that says, "If it ain't one thing, it's another." Most don't even realize that; this quote is made possible by you wakening up every day, opening your eyes and taking a breath. Simply put, just living. My grandfather once told me. "You find men with no problem in only one place, the graveyard." So, understand that each day you are awake and living, every day will not be perfect. Bad things and good things will happen; that's the joy and pain of life.

REVERSE - Real leaders and people of power make their own laws. Not the criminal laws instituted by our government, but mental laws. Laws within themselves that will motivate and guide them to greatness. You have to beware of this ambition because these goals get so addictive that you are blinded by what really matters in life. Like my father once said, "You can't see the forest for looking at the trees." As bad as we all would like to live forever, the sad reality is that we all will die one day, so don't spend your life chasing happiness when sometimes happiness is all around you. Your life!

STORY - My mother, who has always been a very intellectual and instrumental person in her community, is my biggest inspiration. She has always been an avid reader since her youth. She strongly enforced that hobby, skill, talent, whichever you want to call it in me, my brothers, and sister. She always said, "Read, read and keep reading, as much as possible." When I was in school and went home, I read. I had to do homework, and then I had to read at least an hour a day. When I was out of school for the summer or just on breaks, she still made us read at least a book a month. I thought of it as cruel, unfair, and a curse back then. In reality, it was a gift and a blessing. When I got older, I realized reading made me a better talker and thinker and gave me a brighter personality. For that gift, mom, I am forever grateful. Still today, I read a lot, mainly history, business, and self-help. Trying to learn as much as possible about anything to better myself.

Now, I was 12 years old in Thomasville, GA. That year I spent my summer chilling with my cousin Samario at his dad's house in Meigs, GA. When Samario and I found out his Uncle Chilli was growing homegrown marijuana on his dad's side. We discovered this by watching him go to the tool house too many times. We soon found out that he was stashing his finished product there. We begged him for a while about it, and he ended up selling us once for $20. I was amazed at how good the buds looked. The next day I asked him to show me how to grow it. He said flatly no, but I didn't give up. He soon said yes after a week of me bugging him. He said I was persistent and too eager, so he had to show me. First, he showed me how to start a seed growing with a simple wet napkin. I was entrapped when that first day I saw that little root pop out; I was hooked forever. I asked him whether I could see his growing area. He resisted at first, and again my persistence paid off. After a couple of days, he showed me his spot. It was huge! Chillies grow area was located at a creek in the woods by his mother's house. I marveled at the irrigation system and security measures he had put in place. That day Chilli set my young mind to mars, hypothetically speaking. He transformed my mind, and he transformed in my mind beyond a regular man to a mad scientist. I laugh at it sometimes now that I am older, at how drawn in I was at growing marijuana back then at that young age.

That summer, Chilli showed me a lot about growing marijuana back then. The love, time care, growing, curing pollination, and flowering process. I soon got as good as him. I left the next week and went home. I first had to read and research, and then I got better through trial and error. I had to get out there and experiment on my own to fully learn the subject. I couldn't go to the library and get a book on growing marijuana back then. Yes, this is before the Internet. So, I simply asked someone. Their reply was I should read books on herbs, flowers, and horticulture. He said I definitely should learn about growing tomatoes, which puzzled me until I found out that the tomato plant is closely similar to a marijuana plant. Now keep in mind that my father had a lot of land in Thomasville. Now with plenty of wide-open space for me to go and hide my growth. At first, I just randomly planted some seeds in the woods to see the results. Some grew but only to get eaten by rabbits or deer. I guess animals love marijuana too. After a couple of tries, I found the right area, the right security and irrigation. Then I started to grow.

That same summer, I attended a week-long summer camp in

Thomasville. The sheriff's department talked to us about the D.A.R.E program from the second to the last day. They showed us pictures of marijuana growing in the county, to my amazement. The pictures helped me find new ideas of hiding my growth and ways that didn't work. I asked so many questions that day; I laugh now that the officer didn't realize. That I either knew someone growing or was growing marijuana myself. I was a slow criminal back then. I now had about three big plants that yielded around less than a half-pound. The marijuana was okay but not great like Chillies. That summer, I didn't sell but maybe two ounces. I smoked most of it with Samario, Popcorn, and my little cousin Booby and gave the rest away to friends.

One day my parents were gone to a friend's house. So, I decided to check on my two remaining plants. I got on my bike and rode out to the growing area. When I arrived, all of the plants were gone. They had been cut down at the base of the plant. I was pissed; then I remembered the picture I saw of the police raids on grows. Now I was scared to death. I got on my bike and peddled as fast as I could all the way home. I thought the sheriff's department was going to jump out the bushes. That day I thought the sheriff's department was watching me the whole time. I even thought someone had snitched on me. I thought I was about to get arrested. I didn't sleep that night or the next night; also, I was so scared, but by the grace of God, the sheriff never came. I never grew marijuana again outside. I went back to school that year a lot smarter than before. Dealing with Chilli taught me a valuable lesson. You have to study a subject and fully emerge yourself in it. If you want results, it will happen, believe me. This lesson to me was worth its weight in weed!

GAME - I learned early in life that research and homework are very important. By reading, you gain knowledge on a subject and you learn life. With the knowledge, you can learn everything about what interests you. Reading enables you to emerge yourself into a subject.

(1) "Habits are either the best of servants or the worst of masters." Still studying a subject that interests you is the best way to excel in any matter. You can fully know everything about a subject and master it with research.

(2) "No one was born wise." The great Pablo Picasso painted for hours, and then years before he was considered great or even recognized for his talents. Mozart started the piano as a toddler and didn't reach his heights until middle age. The list is endless of people who had to work to get to where they are today. They did that by studying their subjects and putting that research into action. That in itself is proof that by study, research, hard work, and action works. To be great, you have to do your homework and log a lot of time no matter what subject, job, hobby, or plan in your life.

(3) "Knowledge is power" Knowing this is also power, and to gain it is helpful to your road to success. I learned so much about growing marijuana that it amazes people with my knowledge of the subject. I started back studying how to grow marijuana around 2001. Just to learn the newest trick's on growing. I grew a couple of plants trying a new method that I discovered by reading different websites. This process would later prove to be a valuable lesson.

(4) "To know ten thousand things, master one. The others are worthless. First, it will become your habit, then your nature." Suppose I

had not taken the time with Chilli long ago to learn the basics on the subject of growing marijuana and doing my homework. I would have never excelled at buying it or selling it at the level that I did later on in my life.

(5) "There are all kinds of rules that govern behavior, values of good and bad power. A network that must be respected and patterns followed for a successful result. Action if you do not patiently observe and learn them well, you will make all kinds of mistakes without knowing why or how."

Hypothetically, you are an investor on Wall Street or a tech company in California's Silicon Valley. How do you make your money? Let me tell you how; it's simple. You make it by finding what's new, hot and in style. You have to produce a product or invention. For any investor, it's common knowledge that a growing company is what gets you paid.

(6) "Value learning over money." Meaning that you have to find the product first and then research it.

(7) "Understand the real secret, the real power in this world lies in accepting the reality that learning requires a process and this, in turn, demands patience and the ability to endure drudge work." You simply have to do your research to find what's selling. That goes for anything. Suppose you are a clothing designer or a drug dealer. This law goes for anything in the business world. The key is if you work hard, you will obtain it.

(8) "If you are unsure of a course of action, do not attempt it. Your doubts and hesitation will positively affect your execution. Being Timid is dangerous; it's better to go in with boldness. The mistakes you commit

through audacity are easily connected with more audacity. Everyone admires the bold no one honors the timid." To be bold, you have to have confidence and gain confidence; you have to be sure of yourself, the subject, and your moves. The only way to do that is to research and do your homework.

(9) "People who cling to their delusion find it difficult if not impossible to learn anything worth learning. A people under the necessity of creating themselves must examine everything and soak up learning the way a root of a tree sucks up water." To grow, you must learn. Gain knowledge then everything around you will change. If you plant turnips, you will not harvest grapes.

I was employed by the cartel when I was 22 years old. My job was to do the drug distribution's in South Atlanta, GA. Part of my job was to take trips to Mexico to pick out the kinds of marijuana that the market in my area wanted. The cartel never knew that I had that much knowledge on growing marijuana. I always felt strongly that if I hadn't learned how to grow marijuana early, I never would have excelled at doing the job. I chose the plants based on smell, color, seed size, and bud structure. I did some extra research with the growers. I learned their methods of growing and packaging the product.

(10) "Know the other and know yourself, and victory will be total." No matter if the subject is the stock market, painting, woodworking, robbery, or selling drugs. You have to do your homework, to excel in it.

I remember watching the news one day and a young Black man was getting sentenced in court. The judge gave him 10 years on seven counts of aggravated assault. The judge said concurrently that the defendant passed out when he read off 10 years on each count. Simply because he didn't even know what concurrent meant, he thought he had received 70 years. I am willing to bet you; he hadn't spent a day trying to fight his case. That's crazy when you are fighting for your life! When you still won't do the simple homework to save yourself. Do your homework and everything you do in your life will be successful.

(11) "To master any process, you must learn through trial and error. You experiment, take some hard blows, and see what works and doesn't work. In real-time, you expose yourself and your work to public scrutiny. Your failures are embedded in your nervous system; you don't want to repeat them; your success is tied to immediate experience and teaching you more." Learn to study and the world will be yours!

CHAPTER 3

HEAR MORE THAN YOU SPEAK

"One of the most important weapons in the battle for information is giving out false information." **Winston Churchill**

GAME - In the game of power, the truth is a gift and a curse. The truth is sharper than a sword. It could either protect you or lead you to your death. To protect yourself, guard your truths with many levels of lies.

REVERSE - Beware of who knows your truth and who is capable of holding your lies. The closest of friends will betray you with your own truths. Your enemy will only promote lies. Friends tell secrets to hurt you. The truth could set you free or get you a hundred years!

STORY - When I was younger, my mother's grandmother, Ms. Dolli B. Anderson. A sharp, brilliant, elegant woman. Even in her old age Ms. Dolli was as wise as the old owl and as loving as a baby kitten. She had a tiger's heart and anger when crossed. Believe me, that lady didn't play, especially when it came to her family and religion. In her household, you moved by her rules. She used to scold me at times about how much I used to talk. I would never be quiet. My great grandmother and aunts used to laugh at me because they would tell all the kids to be quiet, and I would just keep talking. They always said that I had a lot of words to get out. They or I never realized those words would be through books.

Sometimes when me and my great grandmother were alone and she had time to just talk to me, she would caution, "Chino, God gave you two ears and one mouth, so be quiet, Boy and listen sometimes; you might learn something."

I didn't get it back then, but that saying has always been incorporated in my moves and thoughts. I also incorporated this tactic with legal and illegal transactions with new and old acquaintances. Today, I use this in my day-to-day travels because you really can't trust people!

My first realization that my great-grandmother was on to something came to me when I was around 13 years old. A female named Tameka who had a body like she was twenty-five! She was a baby amazon for real sexy as hell, yet just a couple months older than me, but 10 years more streetwise advanced. She was already experienced in sex and the nightlife. I was still a virgin and curious as hell. Fly as a kite with my social life and dress code. The females loved me, but I was still green as a pool table and twice as square. Don't get me wrong; I've always been on point regarding females. I came from a line of players. Back then, I guess I was just a developing player.

Tameka and I sat beside each other in the back of the class in third-period math. We were kool and besides giving me multiple pussy shots. When she wore a dress, we both would cry laughing at the teacher when she caught him looking too. That school year, she revealed something much better than the mind of a sexually active female. She revealed knowledge. She used to tell me about her sexual escapades on the weekends with different older males. Tameka's mom worked nights, so their house was the spot for the parting late nights. Even better, all the hot females at school spent weekends at her house. Tameka had two sister's one older and one younger. Both were just as fine and sexually active. Every Monday, she had something freaky to tell me. I laughed about it now because I should have gotten at her and got me some sex. Hell, she even told me to swing by her house a couple of times if I was ever on her side of town at night. I guess I was too young to read between the lines back then. She was throwing it at me like a fastball. Trying to let me into her world, and as much as I wanted to, I never had sex with her.

Sometimes I felt I was scared because she was so experienced. I used to listen and get so turned on by her boldness and straight-up freakiness. Sometimes I had to change the subject in our discussions because I couldn't stand up to walk out of my class. My dick was harder than Chinese arithmetic for real. Hell, I even masturbated to the thoughts of her story's before. I can hear all the males reading this saying, "Damn dog, you should have just gotten at her sexually." I just never did and by listening to her, I learned a lot more. I learned a far more valuable lesson than just getting some sex. I learned how to get sex and satisfy a woman when I did get the chance. Tameka didn't realize it, but symbolically, she taught me how to fish instead of giving me food. Also, how to cook it!

She asked me often about my sex life, but I always played it slightly to the left or changed the subject. She was a sweet, kool person. She was very loyal and honest, yet baby girl was just trapped in the hood like me. I never revealed to her I was a virgin. She also never directly asked. She probably figured that I was also sexually active because I held our conversations well, was kinda popular, and had multiple girlfriends. I wasn't sexually active; now that I am older, I see how she could think that. She was wrong! I had not yet completed the mission, but now I was ready!

By listening and learning the things that Tameka had spilled in our weekly conversation. I'm just listening and not running my mouth about it or bragging and boosting like all the lames.

Tameka opened up completely, she felt safe comfortable, and that helped our friendship. It also exposed me to a world that naturally a young male is curious about. She gave me a front-row seat; she taught me the basic fundamental of adolescent sex. I learned so much about what a female's wanted sexually. The gentleness, aggressiveness, confidence, being smove, and the different positions. When I finally did have sex that very same summer. I was so confident that the female didn't even know l lost my virginity to her on my first time. She thought I was a pro and she was a rookie. To this day, she never knew it. I guess until now!

GAME - As I got older, I always loved listening to people before speaking. I learned from my great-grandmother's lessons and applied them. She showed me that it was very important to listen to people first.

Over the years, I found out that listening also gives you a feel for the person you are conversing with. Their true thoughts, ambitions, wants, needs, and ideas. If you listen, then think of a reply; it makes the conversion better and more meaningful for you and the listener. You can apply this, especially in business. Never speak before a person finishes because you might say the wrong thing. The great Napoleon's right hand Talleyrand was a very masterful person in conversation and he was a good listener.

(1) "Talleyrand's ability to suppress himself in conversation to make others talk endlessly about themselves and eventually reveal their intentions and plans. His tactics were like no one else. He fires a pistol into the air to see who will jump out the window." Talleyrand would make those off the wall comments at meetings and dinners to see what other people around him would do or say. Testing them! This skill was classic, yet their actions or comments exposed many of his enemies' cards. Then he would make his moves around their moves.

The Islamic prophet Muhammad was also a good listener. It was said that he would let a person finish talking completely before responding. I feel that was simply because he always got their best response and understood what they were saying better. Then he could morally give his best response. People with pure morals and habits are the best advice-givers.

(2) "What you do not reveal to people is all the more eloquent and powerful." In today's society, people are so concerned with themselves and getting out what they are personally saying, bragging, and boosting or thinking that they are impressing someone. Without knowledge, they are

only exposing their insecurity and faults. Showing their own cards, jumping out the window.

(3) "Oysters open completely when the moon is full and when a crab sees one open, it throws a piece of stone or seaweed in it and the oyster cannot close tightly again. So, then it serves the crab its meat, so is the fate of him that opens his mouth too much and thereby puts himself at the mercy of his listener." Don't be the oyster in this situation; it's better to be a crab.

The usefulness of listening has always guided me through life.

(4) "Never interrupt your enemy when he is making a mistake." When I was about 25 years old, my homegirl Asia first hung a lot with my crew. Well, in Asia's downtime, she kicked it with many baby gangsters and dealers. These baby drug dealers were not on my level in the Atlanta drug game. They did a lot of flexing, trying to impress her and her friends. She always exposed their pillow talk to my crew and me, though. She would always reveal what they claimed they had. Sometimes I would send my little homies to go with her and find out where these flexes for real. Sometimes their pillow talk was correct and the talkers paid the oyster's price, and my team ate.

(5) "All of man's troubles comes from not knowing how to sit still alone in a room." Asia never did want the spoils from the missions. She was just happy to be down with some real gangsters. I always loved her for her loyalty. Unlike other so-called real niggas around me back then, her loyalty never faded. Even during my time in prison, she stayed down. When a lot of others turned their backs, she stood firm.

(6) "When deed speak words are meaningless." It amazes me that

people easily expose their cards with their actions and words.

(7) "The capacity to see the reality behind the appearances is not a function of education or cleverness. People can be full of knowledge and crammed with information but have no real sense of what's going on around them." On the other hand, I have used reverse to this situation of giving out too much information by intentionally giving out false information. I have done this in legal business, but mostly in street business. For instance, I told people I lived in one place and lived somewhere else, or nicknames. I would arrive in town with drug shipment at this time and place, and it would be totally different from what I would tell the customers. Intentionally throwing them off, simply to see if they were trying to rob me or worst, working with the police.

(8) "While spies give you a third eye, disinformation puts out one of their eyes and a cyclops will always miss his target." Disinformation is best a lot of times in the streets and the workplace. You don't want everybody knowing exactly what you are doing.

(9) "Before it is too late, we must wake up and realize that real power and success can only come through mastering a process which in turns depends on a foundation of discipline that we are constantly keeping sharp" Don't slip, stay on point no matter who you do business with.

I learned to talk even less in prison, never about myself, my case, family, business, etc. It didn't matter if you were talking with your homeboys. Still, keep most of your past and present business to yourself. Everybody knows everybody! You will be surprised who you will offend by just talking too much. Believe me, your words could get you killed! I've seen it close up. Listening also keeps people from feeling they know you emotionally. Keeping them out of your weakness. Beware, though, because keeping too quiet scares people, yet it also builds you to be a better person. You will get to know yourself and others will value your own personality, words, thoughts, and decisions. Because now they know you speak for a reason.

(10) "It took this period of forced isolation and repetitive labor to transform him into a genius." Sometimes forced isolation is good for a person and no, I am not saying prison. I am talking about forcing yourself away from all the distractions in your life, good or bad. This isolation triggers your brain to find an activity for you to work on or stay busy with. You must choose an activity that you will use to better you on your road to success, like studying another language, inventing, writing, recording, etc. These activities will soon get mastered with time, forcing you to be better. In my time in prison, I made it my goal to make myself a better man, father, and son. I was building a better me!

PART II

FAVORS

"Don't commit yourself to anybody or anything that is to be a slave to every man... Above all, keep yourself free to commitment and obligations they are the device of another to get you into his power."

Balthazar Gracián

GAME - An old Chinese proverb says, "You ultimately have to give to receive. So, if the willing will receive, then give. When you are receiving back, never let them know. that they are paying a favor back." I always liked this quote because it shows how blessings are made. You gain favor with God, the universe, and your own soul when you help people that need it. Strange as it may seem, the favor, blessing, gifts will come back three times as much if you give sincerely. Try it.

REVERSE - When receiving, always remember that in life, nobody in this world does or gives you anything without looking for something in return. Remember that everything has a cost. It's just a part of life itself. Parents take care of you out of love. Then the hope that one day, you will take care of them. Beware of those that love you for only the things you do for them. Especially if they have this newfound admiration at the brink of your success. Don't be naive; everyone doesn't like you. Find out the reasons the people in your life hate you. You might want to leave most of them alone when you find this out.

LEONARDO DE VINCI

THE LAW OF DILIGENCE

Diligence *(noun)-steady attention and effort as to one's occupation.*

Leonardo De Vinci was born on April 15, 1452. He spent his childhood in Vinci. A small village outside of Florence. His father, Ser Piero De Vinci, was a notary and a staunch member of the powerful bourgeoisie. With Leonardo, fate was born out of wedlock, and by him being the illegitimate son of the notary. He was barred from studying and practicing professional careers such as medicine, law etc. Leonardo received minimal schooling and as a child, he loved to wander in the woods. It seemed to be a blessing to be born illegitimate. That same curse gave him the blessing of freedom and the opportunity to roam. This allowed his natural talent to lead his way in life.

At 14, Leonardo did his first apprenticeship in Florence with Andrea del Verrocchio. Leonardo, in 1472 was admitted because of his remarkable drawings. He was one of Verrocchio's top artists. Leonardo would also contribute to Verrocchio's "The Baptism of Christ." Leonardo also painted "The Last Supper" for the duke of Milan. The duke would later get upset because Leonardo took so long to paint Judas. Leonardo's excuse was because he had to find the perfect model. It was said that he was eager to learn, but Leonardo would soon discover his own talents. Once, it was discovered that he couldn't do the commissions of the rich. He then decided to do something of his own and he invented rather than imitated the rich communist ideas.

Leonardo spent hours experimenting with forms of light and hundreds of variations of shadows. He gave the same attention to the folds of a gown and the expressions of the face. Leonardo would be the first artist to create realistic wings on an angel in a painting. Still, he didn't stop there; Leonardo was obsessed with birds. That is how he came up with the first helicopter model in 1481. The Pope later asked Lorenzo de' Medici to send him his best artist and Leonardo was one of them. At one point, he lived out of the clouds in France as a personal guest of the French king. The king showered Leonardo with money and honors and considered him the embodiment of the Italian renaissance. Soon he would grow tired of Florence and the court politics. Leonardo then made a decision that would change his life forever. He would do what he wanted. Meaning he would pursue all the crafts, science, and anything that interested him.

Leonardo also studied architecture, military, engineering, hydraulics, flight, archery, sculpting etc. Leonardo invented a totally new way of casting iron. Instead of small pieces, he would cast it into sections to make it a seamless piece. For other artists, Leonardo seemed insane for his extreme attention to detail. He received bad attention for this practice. At one point, Michelangelo himself taunted him by saying, "Leonardo made a mold of a new horse you could never see in bronze." Leonardo had a motto of "Ostinato Rigore," Latin for stubborn rigor or tenacious application. He paid everyone no mind. Still living the law of diligence.

Leonardo Da Vinci never gave up on his dreams. He did all his visions on a subject before moving to the next step. What if he had given up on The Last Supper? You would have never seen the Mona Lisa. It is said by countless critics that the Mona Lisa is the most lifelike painting ever painted. That is totally attributed to Leonardo's methods. He was a student of light, shapes, shadows, and colors. His paintings are the most vandalized and copied painting in art history. He was loved for his art but hated because he simply did him. Leonardo Da Vinci is the ultimate example of how it will inevitably pay off if you study any subject thoroughly! The law of diligence.

CHAPTER 4

ALL NIGHT FLIGHT

"The desire to obtain, to aspire is to achieve." **Fredrick Netchze**

GAME - You almost will never lose a woman in the race of life by chasing power and money. The flip side is this; you will always lose power and money by chasing women! You choose; the choice is yours!

REVERSE - The thought that money solves all problems is false, regardless of what the majority of the population believes. Truthfully, money can never buy real love, loyalty, and respect. All those things are earned. If they are bought, watch for the repercussions. One day they will turn on you! Meyer Lansky said, "When you lose money, you lose nothing, when you lose your health, you lose something, but when you lose your character, you lose everything!

STORY - I was around 15 when I started selling crack cocaine. Before that, I only sold breakdown bags of marijuana. I sold mainly to people at my school. My older cousin Blackboy, who started me out into hustling, figured that I would get a better start selling marijuana first. Although I was down for whatever, I still was a little green at the drug game. He picked marijuana instead because the crack game was cutthroat. I only understood this year's later when I got older and into the crack game. Still, back then, I felt he tried my gangster. Selling marijuana taught me the basic rules of hustling drugs. I always had a flair for hustling. That doesn't mean just drugs when I say hustling because you can literally hustle anything. But on the streets, it means getting money without a job. I have always had a good hustler mentality and a dream-like most kids of getting rich. It's ironic that I started with marijuana and ended up with money to burn.

I sold marijuana for about A year before I even touched crack cocaine. I didn't realize back then that crack was a whole different world. Mainly different with the personality of the clientele and also the working hours. I started selling still; I was doing okay, I guess in my book, but my best friend at the time, Romey, also was selling crack. Romey was doing great, though! He was making real paper. He was moving three times as much crack as I was. This puzzled me at first; I couldn't figure out how. We were on the block at the same time. How did he do it! I soon discovered the reason. It was simple; he was clocking three times the hours I was on the block three times. He wasn't at home playing video games watching TV. Romey was on the block! He was on the block until three or four in the morning most nights. He was working extra hard pulling the night shift and sometimes early morning shifts too. Later on, when I got much older, I discovered both were the best times for crack sales. I was still stuck mentally on a marijuana dealer's schedule. Meticulously I devised a plan and eagerly wanted to see how much money I could make. I plotted, planned, and told my parents that I would be attending a sleepover at my other cousin Bone's house on Friday. With a little resistance and negotiations, they said yes. Next, I acquired a G-pack ($1000) worth of crack from my cousin Blackboy on consignment. Now I was ready to get that money.

That next Friday rolled around and I reported to the block around 7:00 for my all-night flight. I normally chased cars as they pulled up to the strip most of that evening. I worked the block mostly, just walking to the store and back. My cousin had a junkie that had a spot on the main street. During those walks, I would also catch plays. I walked to the pool hall and shot pool for about an hour. Willie, who owned the pool hall, asked as I sat eating a chili dog.

"What's up, Lil Chino? You out late tonight; what you got up?" I smiled and told him my plans.

He laughed and said, "One day, Boy, you gonna be rich; you just got to do the right thing with the money and stay buster-free. Stay safe and I wish you luck." He gave me a Coke in a can for free and walked off.

I wasn't into drinking alcohol back then, but my homies Rome and his cousin had a couple of forties. I smoked a couple of blunts with a couple of my other homies, but I was good. I was trying to stay sober as possible. I knew I had to stay on point in the streets even back then. After about 10:00, I mainly just sat in the passenger seat of my cousin Blackboy's car.

He had the classic dope boy old school. It was a metallic blue with silver flake Oldsmobile. He had a white leather interior with blue trim and chrome Dayton's. His car was clean as hell. He used to play the music loud on the block and the hustlers would rap the songs while making bankrolls. Back then, that car was my dream car. I just sat and bobbed my head to the music while my cousin flirted with the females and talked shit to the other dealers. My cousin was a bright light in the hood; he stayed flawless clothes, jewels etc. He was a made man. I could watch my cousin for hours while he operated the hood. I just studied his moves and soaked up the game. The way he moved, handled customers, walked, talked, all the while staying fresh as hell. To me, he was the coldest hustler in the world. When I got older, I hit him up for advice on street shit and crew problems. Big Cuz always held me down with the streets and gave me good advice. For that, I am forever loyal. On that day, around 11:00, he said he was about to go over to some girl's house. He turned the music down and looked over at me with a sly smirk.

"You still staying down tonight, Lil Cuz?"

I proudly replied, "Yeah, what's up?"

He smiled and said, "Kool, I am proud of you for staying down, but Lil Cuz, you ain't got to stay out here all night."

I nodded, "I know, Cuz, but I am good tho."

That little motivation was all that I needed to drive me even more. I now realize he was really worried for me, probably because my mom would have had a fit if something had happened. He kept telling me to be careful. He kept stressing that sometimes undercovers would come through. He was also instructed to watch out for junkies and robbers. He told his homie Slick that worked for him and an older cat named Jojo, to watch out for me and if anything happens to page him 911.

I was now literally ready to rock. We drove to the corner store where we both used the payphone. He called some girl to set up his night. I called my then-girlfriend Nikki to tell her I would talk to her tomorrow. My cousin gave his last instructions, and then he left. I walked back down the street to report for duty. I sold a couple of hand-to-hands most of the night. Then around 2:00, it started to get a little slow. My homie Gator was on the block with me for my first adventure. Everyone else went clubbing, home or out with chicks. I, on the other hand, tonight was determined to sell the full package. I was still wide awake with hope and pride on every sale I made. I had probably $700 in cash. Just knowing I could sell the last $300 in crack. Gator fell asleep a couple of times as we sat on different junkies' porches. Then he finally said he was going home. I walked him home and returned to the block.

That night I would have gone to hell or jail about that thousand dollars. I refused to go in! I just had to win. Walking back to the block from Gator's house, it was now around 4:00 in the morning. Then all of a sudden, it seemed that people just started to come from everywhere. The junkies keep coming faster and faster. I soon ran out of crack.

Jojo and I got a ride to where my cousin was. I woke him up and to his anger and amazement. I gave him his money and I got more crack. I returned to the block and sold like $200 over my goal. That night I sold out in crack. My cousin gave me my percentage the next day. The biggest lesson I learned that night. It wasn't the fact that the late-night crack game was lucrative. I learned that no matter what you do, never stop hustling.

Suppose you have to take a loss or sacrifice a certain thing to obtain your goal. Do it! If that's the case, then that is what it is. Go for it; go hard to reach your goal no matter what happens. Sometimes that is only what is required. A little sacrifice and time.

GAME - In life, you will never understand everyone you meet.

(1) "There are individuals who would rather perish than work, without taking pleasure in their work." I learned that you have to love your work if you want something. Then you have to be willing to deprive yourself of the luxury of certain things to obtain it. You have to choose your weaknesses and decrease them to succeed in life, whether it's sleep, cars, women, the club, whatever. No matter what you feel is holding you back from meeting your goals. Let it go! As long as your goals are met. This is only what matter sometimes most in life.

(2) "There can be no progress or achievements in life without sacrifice, and a man's worldly success will be by the measure that he sacrifices." You have to go on an all-night flight to obtain your goals in life. No, I'm not saying go sale crack all night. I'm saying you have to make the necessary decision and sacrifice. Then sometimes, you simply have to take the chances needed to succeed. Just because you work in a pharmaceutical office and a hustler works the streets. There is no difference. You both want money and you both sell hurtful drugs. There are snakes, rats, and lions in both workplaces.

(3) "The competitive dynamic of the streets and the business world are in fact the same, but your apparently comfortable environment makes it harder for you to see it."

Sigmund fraud once said, "Everything you and I do springs from two motivations sex and the urge to be great." Let me ask you this. What is a failure? A failure only shows you that you had the ambition and strength to try something that no one else had the brains or ambition to do. Success comes after you fail, so you have to keep trying no matter what.

(4) "Everything turns gray when I don't have one mark on the horizon. Life seems simple and depressing. I cannot understand honest men. they lead depressing lives full of boredom." I understand that quote completely. There were many days when I couldn't sleep or couldn't sit still simply because I had no main mission for that day or week.

(5) "Hustle - is staying ahead of your karma" A restless man has no ambition. Even when I got older, I stuck to my guns. I said I wanted to reach a kilo of cocaine in the drug game. I did then; I had five kilos, then 10. I learned that you have to keep raising the bar on your goals. Once you obtain one goal, you have to set another to reach full success. It takes repetition and drive.

(6) "You must act as if it is impossible to fail."

Let's say you want money instead of power. You save thousands of dollars. Then tens of thousands, then hundreds of thousands. Then a half a million, a million and so on. This is very possible. I know because I have done it myself. I remember my little homie Nelly. Who was a big-time trafficker in south Georgia. Told me once, "Bra, you save a hundred thousand; it's easy to save a million.

(7) "The only thing standing between you and your goals is the bullshit story that you keep telling yourself as to why you can't achieve it."

I always looked at my goals and exercise. When working out, you set a goal for yourself. Then when you reach it, you have to raise the bar to get more results. If not, then you will be just exercising just to be doing something. Let's say you start with five reps of push-ups. Then you go to ten in a week. Then you go up and so forth. The next time you do five, you will do it with ease. Before you started, the first rep was a challenge. It's the same with stacking your money.

(8) "Never stop your progress, for more power return to square one psychologically rather than growing fat and lazy with prosperity." Reset your goals. Never settle for less set goals and when you obtain them, immediately set higher ones. Always do better, and more than the last time. This is similar to what Malcolm X was referring to always accomplishing your goals by any means necessary. Achieve it at all costs, whether it's at work, home, school, or in the streets. Go on that all-night flight! Success is a journey, not a destination.

(9) "Most of the important things in this world have been accomplished by people who had kept on trying when there seemed to be no hope at all." Painstakingly I recall that when I was around the age of 25, I was in and out of state a lot, working my ass off distributing drugs to about four different states. I did this all thru people I met thru my connect. I never spent a lot of time at home. This was now causing a lot of issues with my then-girlfriend Simone. That amongst other things she couldn't deal with. It was a constant fight topic, me being gone away from Atlanta all the time. Still, she enjoyed the lifestyle of not having to worry about bills and money.

(10) "America is a capitalist county and I am a capitalist." This means you make, look for and obtain capital. {Money!} I used to take time off still from my out of town moves and kick it with my girl, though.

Regardless of what I did, it still didn't make her happy. Like Jay-Z said in (Song Cry), "Once a good girl gone bad, she's gone forever." I was miserable. I felt when I was at home sitting idle chilling. It was killing my motion in the streets. As time went on, this forced bonding didn't make me or her happy. Then I realized that I was missing money and different business opportunities

(11) "Proverbs say that hard work brings a profit, but mere talk leads to poverty."

I felt I was losing it all behind someone else. It got to the point where I was slightly depressed and upset. I couldn't sleep because I now knew I was shorting myself for her. I soon asked myself why should I do this? Because if she cared about me for real. She would want me to reach my goals in life. She should be happy instead of holding me back.

(12) "There is in this world no such force of a man determined to rise." I had to choose between her or my goals in life. I chose my goals for one simple reason because people will leave you when the fire in your life starts. Whether it's good or bad, never change your grind for someone else. Always choose yourself first and secondly your family. I chose my goals because I needed to get right for my family. My father and mother were getting older and I had just had my first child Samaria. That was the main reason I chose my goals. Strictly to provide for my family. Simone was a painful sacrifice that I had to make on my all-night flight on my road to riches. Sometimes what we think we need in life is all we don't need. The deepest urge in human nature is the desire to be important.

(13) "Only the week rest on their laurels and dot on past triumphs. In the game of power, there is never time to rest." I had a partner that I dealt

with in the drug game named Lil B. He also was from College Park. Lil B, at the time, was making major moves in North and South Carolina. What was ironic at the same time was that he was having all kinds of relationship issues with his girl. It was the same problem I had a couple of years before with Simone.

I told Lil B flatly, "You got to let her go."

He looked at me like I was crazy and he didn't understand. A couple of weeks later, he went to jail for domestic violence and the destruction of property. He had beat her up and fucked up the brand-new Benz that he had bought her. While in jail for those two weeks, his little cousin that worked for him got kidnapped. Lil B had to pay $300 thousand to get him back. When Lil B bonded out, I saw him a week later. I told him he had to be the stupidest, smartest drug dealer I knew. For one, he bought her the car. Secondly, he bought her a new one. What was even sadder was the fact that if he had been home, maybe the kidnapping wouldn't have taken place. Lil B and the girl soon separated. Still, if he had let her go, he would have never gone to jail and saved close to $500 thousand. So never let a person stop you from your goals in life. You can't save or help everyone. My father called people like that slip rocks. Symbolically no matter what you do, they fall down. You can't hold them; they slip out of your hands. If you stand with them, you will slip and fall also. My advice is that when you find these types of people, just don't touch them, or you may slip!

CHAPTER 5

EVERYBODY AIN'T GONNA MAKE IT

"Pick up a bee from kindness, and learn the limitations of kindness."

Sufi Proverb

<u>GAME</u> - Sometimes helping people will ultimately hurt you in the future, more than helping you. You should make finding new friends like trying out for a sports team. Create a list of morals, criteria, and just like a great team, some people will not make the cut. This is how you build your team, not make your team.

<u>REVERSE</u> - Always remember that in life, everyone wears a mask. People only show you what they want you to see. This betrayal of realness has gotten a million times worst with the success of social media. Beware of people masquerading as someone you need or want in your life. Strangely struggles and triumphs bring some of the closest people in your life. Painstakingly, it also brings some of the worst. Try to learn to quickly judge people's character within the first five minutes of meeting anyone. This skill will save you time, money and maybe your life!

STORY - I learned early in life that some people with you wouldn't make it all the way to the finish line. The joy of life is this; there will be some that do make it with you. The reality of it all is. You have to keep in your mind at all times that one day we all have to go to the grave alone. Regardless of how your loved ones feel about it, the fact remains true and evident. Death is the only thing promised with life to everything living on this planet. My father always warned me about the loyalty I had for my friends. He warned how deep in the hearts of men lie deception. He advised that loyalty to my friends and family would haunt me one day. Years later, that loyalty, in a sense, would be a part of the downfall of my empire. That's still another chapter in my life, as well as a lesson in this book.

I was 17 years old; my big cousin Blackboy is the same one that mentored and guided me through every detail of the street life had gotten arrested for cocaine possession. He had received some time in prison. That single circumstance left me with a major grown man issue. First off, it left me devastated mentally. My Big Cuz was my heart; he was family. I felt alone and lost in the streets. Independent, now I had no advisor or safety net. I felt like I was walking the tight rope over the game, at a million feet in the air. Not knowing the future or whether fame was in the cards for me. Would I ball or fall?

Secondly, I had no connect. I felt, either way, I was ready for whatever. It would be many days I walked that tight rope all alone throughout my life. My solitude started to concern my family, not knowing the real reason for my sadness. My father just thought I was sad because my cousin was locked up. He thought that Blackboy was the one buying me all the nice things I had. He never knew it was me and Blackboy was my cover-up. The reason for my sadness wasn't me longing for material things. The main issue was I had no connect for drugs now. Strangely it wouldn't be the last time in my life that I would be faced with that problem.

Freakishly that same year, I lost two more of my friends to the game, besides losing my cousin. One of my homies got charged with murder on some gang initiation ritual. Another one got caught up with some false accusations for rape. It was a situation about a freak who stayed getting trained by the fellas in the hood. Personally, I saw this happen multiple times. Hell, I even ran one on her with the homies one time. She still told her mother my Lil homie raped her because she was pregnant now and didn't know the father. She wanted him to be it and he laughed in her face when she told him. What's crazy is that she could have said I did it because she also liked me. That's some crazy shit, huh. I now count my blessings because he did a lot of time for nothing. That's a real-life situation in a lot of cities all over the world in every hood. My homie got life with no parole for the murder, the other 10 years for the fake rape. Two lives changed forever.

I learned from both situations two major lessons. That changed my path. One was that gang banging didn't add up in the end, and secondly, watch who you have sex with. I felt it was all bad. I was solo; I had to find a connection and fast. I felt like I was just in the first quarter of the game and I had just lost two close friends early in the game. I was down already. It made me angry, but ultimately it also made me smarter.

I had my back against the wall now. So, I started back selling marijuana with my little mix friend Lucus. Lucus's parents had real money. He was kinda spoiled, really. Lucus's dad had a brand new all-white Lexus. The plus for me was Lucas could get his dad's car whenever he wanted. That worked out perfectly for me because I got him to drive me on my moves. I loved that car. I often drove it and that was an instant love affair with Lexus. I promised myself I would get a Lexus one day and I did in 2004. (manifestation) That Lexus was my first foreign car. Lucus and I soon fell out because of business differences. I had the clientele and a small connect through my cousin Shawn's homie Bear.

On the other hand, Lucus had the money or more less access to it. He constantly bugged me to buy into my business. On the other hand, I felt I didn't need or want a partner or a boss. He strongly felt different about our business arrangement. We used to have our little argument over situations because he wanted a better deal on the marijuana and an additional cut on the cocaine business. I laughed at both offers and we argued about it, which was a sign that I should have just walked away then. Still, I was too young to see it.

At this time, I kept good marijuana, not the brown bullshit that most people had. Wishfully Lucus wanted full access to my connect very badly. I felt he had to deal with me still if he wanted it. Ironically at the same time, I started to get a lot of heat from the school administration. A lot of random searches of my locker. The vice-principal even patted me down one morning. Sometimes the police would come and walk drug dogs through the hallways smelling lockers. They never found drugs, though. I never kept drugs on me in school anyway, just money. Nobody but me knew who my drug holder was.

The principal one day revealed to me that he was aware that I was selling drugs at school and even at home. That day, he stood close to me and calmly relayed a threat saying he would catch me soon if I didn't stop. His first mistake made me aware, and now I switched up my operation. Instead of using my usual drug holder, I started to use my then-girlfriend Adrian, which worked out great that opportunity gave her a chance to learn a little about hustling. It was also a blessing because she respected my time with her and away from her more. She learned the time and effort I had to put into my grind. She was a good girl and was great at handling my business. She never sold directly; I wouldn't let her. She used to promote her ass off, though. she would tell different females that her boyfriend had weed and that if they or their boyfriend smoked to buy it from me. She was a loyal person and still today, we are kool as hell.

Shortly after, the heat came; I told Lucus I had to cut down his order, which he didn't like. Next, a couple of days later, he called me at home and said he was kool with the current situation and wondered if I could sell him a half-pound. That was double what he normally coped from me. I asked why so much he said that would help him get through the transition of the price change. Now I immediately had red lights and sirens go off in my head that screamed. Lier!

I could feel the heat in his tone when he replied, "Why you tripping, it's all good," he kept saying, just bring it to school that he had the money.

I replied, "Kool, it was a bet, I gotcha in the morning," and I hung up the phone.

After the conversation, I repeatedly told myself, "Rat, Rat, Rat."

I always knew he was a snake, but I felt I could handle him. He was to me a non-poisonous snake. But like all snakes, they still bite. I kept him close because he spent good money and at the time, I needed him for a lot of different reasons. I always still watched him. With that one phone call, I saw that he figured out my greed and hated his position. But worst, he thought he could take mine. I laughed that he had enough brains to tempt me with money, something that I was after vigorously. He honestly felt I would jump for it asap. He was trying to hang me with my own greed. Except I saw the plan, plain and clear. I studied the situation that day then made my move.

I got up the next day and surprisingly, when I arrived at the school, low and behold, the principal and the sheriff were there to greet me. As soon as I set foot on the property, I saw him smile when we locked eyes.

He asked, "Can I search you?"

I replied, "Yeah."

But before he did, I handed him a card that I had bought the night before. The card had a cake on it and in big red letters "Congratulations." When he opened it and read his name at the top, I also mentioned Lucus during the letter. He looked as if he wanted to tackle me right in front of the police. He just smiled, though and reached for my bag. While the police patted me down, I stood silent as the other students watched, figuring I was caught up. They found nothing. The cop then flexed his muscle a little, talking tuff, but they let me go. I realized two things with that search. The first being Lucus was a rat for real and he had to be dealt with properly. The second lesson was the value of a little information. The simple movement and placement of misinformation will change the game completely.

Lucus angrily realized his plan hadn't worked when he saw me posted on the wall with my homies an hour later. I was laughing and having fun. The expression on his face was priceless! He looked as if he had seen a ghost. I laughed, but I was heated inside like boiling water. I could easily have beat him up and he knew this. I didn't want him to know how pissed I was inside at him. I know that scared him even more. I just wanted him to know that I was smarter than him. I wanted him to know that he also was a rat bastard. He still had knowledge of my business moves outside of school, so I had to play it kool. I devised a plan to push him further away but slowly.

I took like $200.00 worth of marijuana and paid two different gang members that I knew to keep pressuring him at school after a couple of missed payments from his customers and beatings. The gang member even broke the windows out of his dad's Lexus one day, which I hated to see. Still, I felt it was mandatory to get the point across. He soon relocated to another school. I was told this move was not because he wanted to. People said his parents felt he was unsafe. He eventually called me and asked for help because he knew I had gang connections. I acted as if I couldn't help, though. He revealed that the gangs were pressuring him even at the new school and he couldn't sell weed there. I told him I would see what I could do. After the conversation that day, it amazed me that he still couldn't see that I was the one sending the pressure. Eventually, I weaned him away like a baby from a bottle. I never saw Lucas again.

GAME - I once read a quote in an Islamic self-help book that stuck with me.

(1) "He who has slacked his thirst immediately turns his back on the

well no longer needing it." Symbolically means once you have gotten what you want from someone, people leave. I know a lot of people out there with Lucus-type people in your lives or circle. You have hater's that want to bring you down as my vice-principal did. You have people like the cop that wanted to catch me at the school. He didn't even know me and hated me. The joy of life is this you also have people like my cousin Blackboy, my ex-Adrian trying to help you win in life. This is another lesson you must learn early in life to discern friend or foe, or you will pay a price. That price most are not prepared to pay.

(2) "Do not imagine that your masters' dependence on you will make him love you. In fact, it may make him resent you and fear you. It is better to be feared than loved. Fear you can control, love never. Love is changeable; fear will never change." You have to learn to make the best and accept the worst of both of these types of personalities because some things in human DNA will never change.

I have a friend who was in one shoot-out and went to prison for life at 16. I have friends who have also died in shootings and robberies at that same age. I've seen people get on highways with drugs for the first time and get locked up, or even worst, killed in a different state during robberies. In the streets, there will be multiple situations. Some will go to prison and some will go to the grave. It's crazy when both were just trying to feed their families. Imagine just trying to get money for diapers or milk for your kids and you get killed. I've read situations that have happened in three strikes states like California, where people get 40 years for stealing milk and diapers: that's crazy but true.

(3) "Reality has its own powers; you turn your back on it, but it will

find you in the end, and your inability to cope with it will be your ruin." I am about to say now that I am not trying to brag, boast, or glorify street life. Still, I've done multiple crimes in different states and survived them all. I feel strongly that Allah wants me to tell this story to change someone else's life. I've seen my friends get life sentence after life sentences for all kinds of crimes. I've also seen the bodies of the innocent laid to rest before their time. It's fucked up for real, yet a part of the game. I don't condone none of it. Still, it's there and we have to deal with it every day. I've seen big-time street players, killers, and robbers get on the inside of a prison and fold like a kitten. I've seen grown men beat until they have feces spread all over the dorm. You will never know who is real and who is fake by talking. Pressure brings the truth to all human characters.

(4) "And an enemy who does not respect you will grow bold and boldness makes even the smallest animal dangerous."

With all of my trials in life, I deeply feel that I am only here because of Allah's (God's) grace. So please, at no time think that I am bragging or showing off. This book is proof that it was propelled by something bigger than me and you. (Predestination) My personal thought is that I can save someone's life, child, or father. Preventing them from serving time and it destroying their lives. Ultimately keeping the mental chains of slavery on them. Please don't judge my story; just read the lines carefully. Take away the struggle and pain from the stories of my life. Find joy in my ups and downs. Be glad elated when I speak on the lessons and jewels I have gained as a man. See the changes instead of the negativity of my life. See the footprints in the sand through my eyes. See what I saw in my own future.

I remember riding through downtown Atlanta in the passenger seat of my homie named Blue's brand-new Hummer H2. The truck was black, with a brown leather interior, sunroof, and all. Blue had just put rims on it earlier that day before we went out. Bra had hella cars, a Monte Carlo on 26's, Grand Prix on 24's, and like five other old schools that were his hobby, 'addiction whatever you want to call it, but that's what he loved to do. Hell, most of my homies did that; I felt it was too hot to keep coping cars. Like I said, my addiction or hobby was jewelry. Blue was a close friend and I still call him my brother to this day. That day we were coming from the club celebrating because we just made a clean $278,000 in one week, on top of what we paid his connect back. I won't say how, but I will say there was a room, a re-rock machine, me, and Blue with 10 bricks. At this time, it was a drought, drought in the city; we turned one's into four's that day. Blue still is and forever will be one of the best I ever saw work a re-rock machine. Pulling into my driveway, we sat for a minute and we both rolled blunts, just talking.

I remember the thick weed smoke running out of the sunroof as I asked him, "Bra, where do we go from here, like how much more do we need? Hell, we secretly had the southside on lock what was next for you."

He smiled and lit the blunt back up and said, "I want the world for us Bra and everything in it, and if you ain't our family, then Bra, they are in the way."

Back then, I wasn't fucking with a lot of people and Blue had shown through his actions he was a real friend time and time again. What he said that night mentally stuck in my head ever since that day and I built my team on that motto silently in my head for years. Someone had to show me he was family; if not, you were on the other side. Blue ended up catching some time, but we laughed at the old days when he got home. Now I had a legal business and was getting 18 wheelers of weed in back-to-back. Blue was a pure friend back then and he still is La Familia today. Sometimes the people who love you do love you.

(5) "The key to life is always be willing to walk away." Beware of the enemy that comes with a smile; he is much more dangerous than the one with a pointed weapon.

(6) "People who praise you too much or become too overly friendly in the first stages of knowing you are often envious and are getting closer, only to hurt you." It is sad to say, but in the game of power, you have to watch your friends and family because, like my father always said, "Everybody ain't gonna make it."

(7) "There are little friendships in this world and least of all between equals." Just remember that the small enemy may be your girlfriend, best friend, cousin, business partner, etc. Anyone that you have overlooked simply because of their smiles or gentle gestures. All the while, their anger and hate are growing stronger inside and the closer they get to you, they gain power. This transforms them into a bigger opponent, giving them more ammunition to bring you down. Simply because you have underestimated them, resulting in a situation that you thought you could handle, but in the end, you couldn't.

(8) "Beware of feedback from friends whose judgments could be tainted by a feeling of envy, or the need to flatter." Again, the best advice is your own. Don't be afraid of the enemies who attack you. Be afraid of the friends that flatter you. I've played the sheep before in my quest to

power; we all have. The difference is while I was the sheep, I was sharpening my claws and teeth, waiting for the perfect time to strike like a cobra. I've played the lame. The chauffeur, Lil homie, the goffer, all position in my rise to power. I've even acted dumber than the person in control of the situation or business. I was just waiting for my opportunity to present itself, then to strike. I've always been cautious of new people I run into in the streets. That's has been one of my natural habits, other than my flare for business opportunity and just finding money out of nothing. I found that lying dormant like an alligator is one of my best characteristics.

(9) "Be polite, be professional, but have a plan to kill everybody that you meet. In other words, make friends out of potential enemies." Always be on point. Sometimes acting like you are not a shark, but you are. That way you can swim with the dolphins and eat.

(10) "Abraham Lincoln's choices were pure pragmatism; he was a keen observer of human nature and stuck with Ulysses S. Grant because he was the only general capable of effective action. He judged people by the result, not friend lines or potential veins." Actions speak louder than words always. Learn this tactic fully so you will recognize it even if slightly tempted when it is tried on you. Reverse their tactics and try it on others sometimes because acting like a lion is the way to learn the moves of a lion. Portray him then you will see why he does what he does.

(11) "The sense of having doubters, or enemies can serve as a powerful motivation device and will propel you with and added creative energy and focus." Feed off the haters! Let it motivate you by learning to hide your steel fist inside a velvet glove. Only revealing it until it is time to strike the fatal blow. You will reveal it when your opponent doesn't

realize that their fate is sealed and they have no option but to take the blow. This is beautiful when executed correctly; this is a great tactic, but you have to have the patience to lay and wait like the great alligator. Just waiting to release your rath at the right time. Remember this quote;

(12) "If you go looking for friends; you're going to find they are very scarce. If you go out to be a friend, you will find them everywhere." So, learn to plan for the future build your team of friends with caution. Remember this, the game of life is chess, not checkers!

CHAPTER 6

JUNGLE LAW
THE GAZELLE GETS EATEN BY THE LION

"Learn to tell the Lion from the Lamb or pay the price."

Niccolò Machiavelli

GAME - One day in the jungle, a lion meets a tiger, and as they drink beside a pool of water, the tiger asks the lion, "Tell me, why do you stand over there in the morning and roar like a fool?"

"That's not foolish," said the lion, "they call me the king of all the beast because I advertise."

A rabbit sitting in the bush overheard the conversation and thought he would try the lion's advice. The rabbit began to roar, but it was only a squeak when he did his roar. So, he kept trying. A fox heard the multiple squeaks and came to investigate. Then he had himself the rabbit for lunch in the woods! The moral of the story, my friends, is this. Be sure you got the goods to back it up when you advertise!

REVERSE - In life, sometimes people may think that you are soft because you don't advertise danger. They don't see the danger and they mistakenly agitate you. Lions and bears roar. A rattlesnake rattles. A fox and alligator are silent. Elephants stomp and make a loud noise to show you he is dangerous. Nevertheless, a black widow is small and silent, yet one of the deadliest things on this planet. Strangely the loud ones are not the ones to be afraid of. The deadliest one in the room is the silent one waiting on you to slip then hurt you. This is the one to watch!

This chapter will symbolically refer to the different human characteristics and class them with certain animal characteristics. This is strictly my own opinion and I hope no one takes offense. Try to picture people in your life that fit these comparisons. Hopefully, you will figure out how to handle them to your benefit.

ANIMALS

1. GORILLA: Gorillas are easily manipulated; they think their size and strength make them better or uniquely empowered over certain things. They try to throw their weight around. They are also violent, normally non-thinkers.

USE: If you find a chimp with more brainpower, they can use a gorilla as muscle or to apply pressure and fear where it is needed. A gorilla is easily manipulated.

BEWARE: Of a gorilla that is a thinker. This is rare and very dangerous. If betrayed, a gorilla is a dangerous and violent foe. If he finds out that you are manipulating him. He will hurt you, so hide your moves well or pay a price when handling the gorilla personality.

2. ALLIGATOR: Alligators are lazy and mostly wait on their food to cross their path rather than go hunting. It will hunt if needed, though. They are very vicious and dangerous if provoked.

USE: An alligator is an easy piece to acquire. Still a valuable piece on the team. Because you feed an alligator and when needed, you call on them strictly for violence. Place an alligator in your territory and he will defend it to the death if trespassed.

BEWARE: Alligators are very territorial. Give them their space but watch them because your territory will become theirs in their minds. You have to keep reminding them that they are just holding the territory for you. You do this by holding close to what makes them work for you. (The food)

3. <u>ZEBRA</u>: Zebras blend in with the crowd and different surroundings. If accompanied by a gorilla or wolf, a zebra will act dangerous. All the while, they are scared prey.

USE: A zebra is good for finding information on other people, or crews, by using their stripes to blend in with the enemy's surroundings. You could send a zebra out of town and he will blend in and report back to you.

BEWARE: A zebra's timidness could be fatal when exposed or threatened. If you have a zebra working for you, use it with caution. If threatened with danger from an enemy. He will tell everything he knows about you for their own safety. Keep their knowledge limited. On a need-to-know basis because they can only tell what they know.

4. <u>RABBIT</u>: Rabbits rely on their speed to maneuver in and out of dangerous situations. They are very timid and suspicious of anything that might threaten their lives.

USE: You can always use a rabbit's timidness as an alarm for danger. His speed and trickery to do your work behind enemy lines. Use his ability to get in and out safely.

BEWARE: A rabbit will surely run away from you if they are scared. So be very gentle when dealing with them. Never put all of your faith in a rabbit. They're born to run!

5. <u>SNAKE</u>: Snakes can lie on the bottom and not be seen. This is a very useful skill because they are very deadly. A snake is a master deceiver and trickster. A natural at low life conning. A snake has no loyalty, only to himself and his needs.

USE: A snake can get into most places most cannot. They are ready and willing to do all your extra dirty work, so let them. Snakes are great at lying, tricking, and conning. They are not so much of a killer, though. Some will, if needed or threatened.

BEWARE: As you feed a snake, it will try to trick, eat, even bite you as the handler. It takes years of training to become a snake charmer for a reason. If rubbed slightly wrong, a snake will react and bite you. Or do something worse to hurt your future plans. Play with your snakes at your own risk.

6. WOLF: Wolves are violent, dangerous, and usually, they run in groups. The group relies on a hierarchy and their reputation to scare you. Wolves don't hide; they show they are in an area by howling and showing off.

USE: Enforcers, they will keep people away from you. The big plus about employing a wolf is they come in packs. If you employ the alfa wolf, you run the pack also. They are great for hunting prey and also defending territory.

BEWARE: A wolf will kill whatever shows signs of being hurt or weak. Beware if you are falling from grace or prosperity. Don't expect a wolf to save you. It will eat you!

7. ELEPHANT: Elephants possess great wisdom and knowledge and are good listeners. An elephant is a person that you call on for knowledge. They listen well and are good information keepers and seekers. They are people you trust and rely on. When times are bad and you need good advice. They are strong, loyal, and lifelong friends.

USE: Consigliere, when you have a decision to make, the elephant will be a good person to talk to. They will give you an honest and strong opinion.

BEWARE: There is no fear of you because they know all your strengths and weakness, and the elephant will turn against you if provoked. If they do, they are very dangerous. The only way an elephant will betray you will be provoked by your betrayal and miss deeds against him.

8. <u>SHEEP</u>: A sheep is very loyal until they feel unprotected. Then they will try to protect themselves by finding security in someone else. Sheep are no threat for danger.

USE: Information. The shy timidness is a good thing for you. Sheep will report all threats and dangers in the area simply out of fear of getting eaten themselves. Always remember you can shear a sheep a thousand times, profiting by selling the wool, or you can kill him and eat once. Tell a lone sheep all of your misinformation and it will get to your enemy's ear quickly.

BEWARE: Only for the use of misinformation. A sheep is not a killer or confidant. They may associate themselves with one sometimes. If threatened or for various protection reasons.

9. <u>LION</u>: A lion rules his kingdom. He is the king and boss. The ultimate alpha in the area. A lion rules by fear, knowledge, violence, and dependence.

USE: A lion will eat it or use it as a worker when faced with a lessor opponent in life. A lion can be a useful ally or a fearless foe in their game of life, only to another lion.

BEWARE: Respect the warning in the roar of a lion. It will defend itself to the death or devour you!

STORY - By the time I was 19, I had seen twice as much as a regular 19-year-old with all the drugs partying, violence, losses, and chasing women. I started running in and out of state, trying to move drugs. I stayed for short stints in Virginia, Mississippi, Chicago, and Florida. All by the age of twenty. I tried working; it didn't work out for me. I had my high school diploma, but due to restrictions for disciplinary actions. I didn't get a chance to walk at graduation. I got kicked out for throwing a badass skip party with a lot of the school in attendance. That I felt hurt my parents more than me, they were the ones who dragged me thru those years when I felt school was lame. Hell, I even thought about a life in the military and leaving the hood all behind me. I still chose differently. I even had to serve a little jail time in Mississippi and Virginia. I was really just trying to find myself and my way in this crazy world back then. While in Virginia, I had gotten into some trouble with the police. My father and brother advised me to come home. They both feared I would have gotten into some real trouble and never see Georgia again. Hell, I almost did. Then I decided to take their advice.

In 2000 I left Virginia and returned back to Georgia. This move broke my then-girlfriend Diamond's heart. As I got older, I felt she still was another sacrifice to my road to greatness. I had already learned that in this game, you have to never put your feelings over money and your goals sometimes. If you don't, you're in the wrong game and you should stop now! Get a job now! Just square up and quit. The streets ain't for you.

When I was in Virginia serving jail time, my brother Shannon moved back to Atlanta. During this time, one of the most painful and joyful events of my life happened.

My nephew Daishawn was born. It was painful because he almost died. I prayed for days and cried for nights. Ultimately, I trusted that it was in God's hands and he walked my Lil man through it. It's crazy because I thought I had it all figured out back then. In all reality, I didn't have a clue in the world about what I wanted in life. I just knew one thing. I couldn't take being broke and depending on other people.

Let me take a second to tell you about my character as a hustler. As far back as I could remember. I have had a very special love affair with money. Since I was a youth, I had to have something going on to get some money. If I didn't have money. I couldn't eat or sleep. I don't know how I got like that. As a youngster, I used to stay up all night dreaming about money, cars, houses, etc. I have always wanted to fix or better my family's situation. At this time, I was broke. I had just fought a case in Virginia and was now back in Atlanta. This financial embarrassment was driving me crazy. By all means, I wanted to square up for my family and get a job, but it seemed like every corner I turned, the jungle was calling me back on a loudspeaker.

I meet Fateta in Atlanta thru my best friend Javon's sister Nicole. Our relationship was strained from the start. I was back at it, living a wild lifestyle, drugs, robberies etc., trying to get it together. Back then, I was extra wild. What amazed me was that she understood, loved, and respected me. I went back to jail during our relationship for a probation violation. I had to do like six months in Clayton County. To my amazement, she stayed down the whole time. She was a great friend first, then girlfriend. She has always been a positive and good person in my life.

When I met her, she had a one-year-old son and was trying extra hard to make it just like me in this crazy world. It wasn't easy being a single mother trying to provide for her son. I respected her a lot more for that alone. She didn't do hood hoe bullshit. She was a good girl. She still went to school and stayed down until she graduated. Then she went back to school until she found her passion and her grind. I strongly felt back then I was fucking her life up with all of my street shit. She would do anything I asked her. She never asked, from picking me up after drug deals, robbery's, etc. I loved her so very much. That I had to let her go, I felt she was too good of a girl for that life. So, for her and her son's sake, I let her go. I had to let her find the right direction in her life. I felt my life back then was way too wild for her. We never stopped talking or seeing each other. She still is one of my closest friends. I've always felt our love was a sacrifice I had to make. It hurt like hell, believe me. I had to watch her have boyfriends and shit!

LOL, What makes this story so important is that God brought her closer to me, with her giving me a beautiful little girl named Emani. How well that's another story in another book. I met Simone around the same time Fateta and I first split. She was the Jamaican wildcard that I didn't see coming. I should have left her alone from the start and just stopped the street shit and stayed with Fateta. But like most men, we choose the worst option for the worst reasons. I should have left when Simone first showed signs of disloyalty. Still, you live, love, and learn. That's just life; we all go through these struggles and situations. That's the joy of love and life.

At this time, I was working a little marijuana. Nothing major two or three pounds and doing small-time robberies and scams. Eating symbolically (rabbits and zebras), nothing major. I was back in the hood and tripping without a map. I also met my partner Cory at this time. He had just moved to Atlanta from Memphis. He was a real hyena ass nigga! He was wild as fuck. Cory didn't give a fuck about nothing. His wild ways and my train to go ego keep me in some bullshit. I soon got the reputation for slanging that iron (shooting people) on the southside. I was revered as a young wolf. I would later need a reputation in my resume as an enforcer for my first major connect.

My older cousin Blackboy was now in prison for the second time and ironically, I was still lost in the game, trying to find my way. My cousin T was selling crack in the west end at this time with our close friend Goldie. Goldie was a real boss. A lion on the streets. I started hanging at their trap a lot. They both knew I was a wild gunslinger, but mostly I was family, and I was the youngest, so it was kool. I mostly just hung around. I wasn't really selling crack or hustling; I was just chilling at their spot smoking and talking shit. They didn't know Cory and I was robbing the whole southside at night. I was stressing about life period. I didn't feel the hunger to hustle. I just wanted to take. I felt my cousins needed me around for security, but they never said so. They were making good money at that spot. I just couldn't find the motivation to grind. I had lost it somewhere. I just kicked it with the crew most of the time. The rest of the time I spent in Riverdale with Simone.

Goldie was kinda my second mentor in the drug game. He liked me around a lot. I always thought Goldie saw a lot of me in himself. He never knew I gravitated to him because I saw a lot of my cousin Blackboy him. The way he moved and controlled the block. T and Goldie kept me smoked out and calmed; they even would feed me some days. Hell, Goldie even took me shopping before. Big Homie looked out majorly back then and for that, I would have given him anything. Now and then, Cory and I would hit a good lick (robberies). It would be maybe five to ten thousand.

I would just blow the money on bullshit. Small moves but lifesaving at the time. I felt Goldie did all those things to keep me close to him, so I didn't do anything dumb and ended up in prison for life. A lot happened that year, too much to even talk about. I could never discuss a lot due to the statute of limitations on certain crimes. We got it how we lived back then. Straight out the mother fucking mud! Goldie showed me a lot about the street from a lion's view. I will forever be in his debt for life for that. Goldie went to prison the next year in Tennessee for murder and attempted murder. He received a sentence of life plus 65 years.

All because he was a lion and some hyena tried to rob him. He handled his business as a man and shot back. Ironically that same situation I would face 10 years later. After the shooting in Tennessee, Goldie went on the run in Atlanta. I begged him to let me help with his snitch problem, which was to testify at his trial. He flatly said no every time. He said he wanted to face it straight up. He wanted to see the rat and hyena on his own terms. Goldie was a solid person, a real gangster. I would have rocked the rat to sleep for Big Homie for free and he knew it. I felt he didn't want me to get caught up. A lot of big homies would have sent me on that mission to help themselves. Yet, he declined for my safety. He didn't give the green light and at the trial, they gave him life.

After his trial in Tennessee, and T and I went back to the west end. Devastated in Atlanta, we both felt lost and posted up in Goldie's trap. I felt I had to keep the trap rocking for Goldie and his street legacy. Many people felt it was free territory now that Goldie was in prison. Goldie was the lion and T was his lieutenant, a young tiger. Still, he was not the lion. Back then, I was the wild card that nobody saw coming. Simba, the heir to the throne. Back then, people said I acted like Joe Pesci on Good Fellas. I see it now and laugh. I did have a hair-trigger and a violent temper. They never understood I was just doing me.

One night about a week later, we returned to Atlanta from Goldie's trial in Tennessee. I was out on the block doing my part for our team selling rocks holding the trap down. A tall man with dreads pulls up in a black Cadillac Escalade. A real gorilla ass dude symbolically. So, this dude starts talking shit about Goldie. Acting like a gorilla, charging with his head down, not seeing that he was about to hit a brick wall. He sat there yapping about real estate and territory. He voiced that he felt he was the lion on the block now that Goldie was serving time. I snapped! We then have some words; let's just say I felt I couldn't let him play my team or me. He kept talking and I lost my thought and got mad. I stop talking and start walking back to our trap house.

I walked in the spot and told T, "Let me get the choppa." Him and my homie Lil T looked at me crazy.

They both ask simultaneously, "What for?"

I explained the situation and they both agreed it was go time. We go back down the street and air out the whole block (shot up) the gorillas trap. The gorilla got the message and he ended up not coming back to the jungle ever. He called the cops on us in the end, though. I heard later from a chick that lived in that neighborhood that he went back to his side of town in east Atlanta. To this day, this guy is a well-known hustler in

Atlanta. Again, that's another story in my life.

A couple of weeks later, I got the chance to talk to Goldie on a call from prison. I explained the situation. I thought he would be proud of me. He totally did the opposite. He yelled at me and got mad. I couldn't figure it out. He was mad at me for bussing my gun. He then explained that he didn't want me to end up in prison for some bullshit. He said he knew the gorilla and that we did right to handle him. He just didn't want me to get into trouble. He explained that the gorilla was a chimp, trying to act tuff to trick me. That's when Goldie revealed something to me that has always stayed with me since he said it.

He said, "Cuz the streets are ran by jungle law, the gazelle gets ate by the lion, so hold it down with an iron fist. Just know when to attack. Be smart; don't hesitate or play with the other animals out there; everyone is hungry."

I always respected Goldie. He was a real hustler and killer. Still an original gangster, a rare combination of smarts and strength. I took what he said to heart and to the top!

I then start using my knowledge and strength to hold things down other than my gun. Shit was still crazy; T was getting ready to go to trial in a couple of months for a shoot-out we had gotten into in Clayton county. As I said, back then, it was a very fucked up and wild. I might see the wrong person at a store, mall, etc., and it would go down right then. It was a lot of robberies and drug deals have gone wrong to our benefit. I didn't give a fuck; the jungle law was in full effect. Gazelle, rabbits, bears, whatever got eaten. We were out there getting it in for the team, however. We had to get T a lawyer and money for Goldie's appeal. It was all kinds of bills and problems. I was also dealing with relationship drama. I was stressing like hell!

Here I am, 20 years old, not even legal to drink. I felt like the whole world was on my shoulders. My cousin T trial finally rolls around and they railroad him. He kept it solid in this instance and didn't mention my name. He took his time like a G. that time. Now I was again solo. My uncles, aunts, and friends around me began to tell me to hold my head and stay focused. T and Goldie even called and said, "Don't spaz out!" I was too close to almost snapping and doing some crazy shit. I had planned solo with an armored truck. My crazy homie from Memphis Cory was down with it. My Lil homie from bank head courts T-bone talked me out of it.

He said, "It was a lot of people out here that was happy that my team was fucked up. Chino, the street is waiting on you to do some dumb shit and go to prison too."

When he said that, all I could hear was Goldie in my head saying, *don't play yourself off the streets, and the gazelle gets eaten by the lion.* I still go on a robbing spree all over Atlanta for the next 30 days. Everything and everybody was prey. I first robbed one person for a half kilo to get the trap back moving. Then I called up some of Goldie's old connects and partners. One of them was Lil Tauren. He was a slick cat as greasy as oil on plastic. Goldie told me to keep my eye on him a long time ago when he was out.

He said, "Lil T couldn't be trusted; the right thing he will switch up on you," he smiled, "believe me, Lil Cuz, he too slick for his own good."

I didn't care. I felt he was an alligator, too slow and dumb to trap me. I was a young lion and I hunted for my food. His ass would end up on the plate, too, if he played.

A week after I first talked to Lil T, he called me and said he had a move for 60 pounds of marijuana. Now in my mind, it was a go regardless. Still, I was a little skeptical and shaky because Tauren was slick for real. At this time, it was still a lot on my plate. I had mega bills that I needed to handle. I called Lil T back and said fuck it let's do it. Two days later, we met up with the seller downtown. Lil T's job was the middle man; I was the buyer/robber. This lame finally pulls up.

When I see him, I smile. He was a real zebra. He gets into my car and we start talking. He looks at my jewels, watch, chain etc. Now he feels comfortable (that's why I borrowed it). I showed him the fake bag of money and he just nodded. We then get out of my car and walk to his truck. There were three dog food bags with marijuana in them. In my mind now, it was go time. There was only one problem. I had to figure out how to get the marijuana in my trunk first. I get him to help me put them in the trunk with a little finesse. What's crazy was I still hadn't given him a dime or the fake money bag. As soon as my trunk closed, I pulled the chrome S&W 45 out of my waistline. He sees the gun and immediately starts to run away, screaming, "Don't shoot!" A typical zebra. I laughed, jumped into my car, and left.

An hour or two later, Lil T calls me and says, "Bra, the people I robbed all of a sudden now knows where I stay at and they are about to shoot up my house, but if you give me the marijuana back, I will take care of it and take it back. Then everything would be kool."

I laughed and hung up the phone. Then I laughed harder when I thought about it later that night in the robbery game. Nothing but the triple cross will beat the double-cross. This fool thought I was that stupid or dumb to give him back the marijuana. Lil T was around 26 years older and I just turned twenty a couple of months before this, but he never knew that I had never been dumb or slow. Truth be told, at first, I had all intentions of honoring me and Lil T's original agreement. I was supposed to give him 30 pounds of marijuana from the deal. He now played himself with his own greed. Typical small-minded alligator shit. He messed up his whole share by not respecting his own word. Now instead of me having 30 pounds, I had the whole 60. I took a day off and got a room to relax. That day I thought to myself, *"T was locked up and so was Goldie doing life in another state. I needed to do this right to come up for real. I take the marijuana to my female cousin's house and hide out at my brother's spot for a couple of days, to think."*

I sent Goldie and T some money on their books. Then I wholesaled 20 pounds to get some start-up money for my plan. I called Simone, my then-girlfriend and asked her should we move in together. I then explained that I needed a base. I really needed a backbone, someone to trust. I told her I needed a strong woman and friend beside me to get through what I had planned. I made a promise to her that with God's help, I would show her the world and more. All she had to do was stay down with me through whatever came. Sometimes I think back to that day and I figured that was a major mistake. Again, I should have moved in with Fateta and just changed how I lived. Still, I also loved Simone, and I felt she was someone I could trust.

She smiled a big bright smile and said, "Yes, Baby, I would love to and I got you no matter what."

The next week I moved back to College Park. The reason I chose this story was because of the lessons I learned and also its importance. Because with that single move for those 60 pounds and Tauren's greed. That was the spark that I needed and it got the fire started. I remember reading a long time ago,

GAME - (1) "That to masquerade as a swine is the best way to eat a tiger. The easier it is for him to think he can prey on you; it is far easier for you to prey on him." Attentively you have to take a moment and try to look deeper into this quote. First, you have to look at the life of a swine which is dirty and lowly. Still better, this quote shows you the level of deception one has to go through to get to their targets. This characteristic is hard for some and some natural. Now for an example. Have you ever taken a real look at a house cat's movements? Have you ever seen how he stalks his prey? In that alone is proof that it's in their DNA. They hunt the same way as a panther, tiger, or lion. They stalk their prey and ponce on them.

(2) "The hunter does not lay the same trap for a wolf as for a fox. He does not set bait where no one will take it. He knows his prey through their habits and hideaways. He then hunts accordingly." This is very true. In the jungle (the world), you have different animals around you. Predators and prey. You cannot hunt a drug dealer the same way that you would robber, Ponzi scheme or any other criminal. In the same way, you cannot hunt a wolf, as you would a turkey or rabbit. For one, when scared, the wolf will defend his life to death. A turkey or rabbit will only run away. So, know who you are dealing with a wolf or a turkey. What's amazing is that with a little homework. In life and in the wild, I discovered

a wolf is a lot easier to kill than a turkey. When hunted, the proper way, you can kill a wolf with a single blade and a drop of blood. A human with a wolf mentality and a real wolf will kill themselves with their own greed.

Mankind can calculate the movements of the stars, but not the madness of men. These rules apply to the people in your circle. Either legal or illegal, you have different animals and you have to handle them differently. Have you ever just sat back and studied the people around you? Have you tried to classify them according to your liking? If you are a gazelle, you don't want to run around with lions. Because sooner or later, you will be food unless you keep serving your greater purpose, which you need to find. In the game of life, you always want to be the one calling the plays. The coach instead of the one in the game executing the play or getting the play ran on them. Beware of the other wolves in sheep's clothing or swine's masquerading trying to kill a tiger. Remember that people are like fish in the ocean, some people like to operate on the bottom, sharks etc. The simple, pack swimmers live on top and often are as food.

(3) "It's not the strongest of the species that survives nor the most intelligent it's the one most responsive to change." Often in the jungle, you will run into crafty foes. When your life is lived on this level, you have to craft and end game. You have to learn to detect the signs in people quickly. Before they detect who you are and your real purpose for being around them. I believe that there are no mistakes in life, only lessons to learn. There are billions of people in this world as well as billions of personalities. People are very different in many ways, except there are a set of deep characteristics that you will find in a lot of people that you can

put into categories. You cannot treat everyone the same, even the people you put in your categories. You have to approach everyone differently. You have to learn that certain people are prone to certain actions and habits. So, study them and then you can put them into slots in your own mind.

(4) "Nobody gives you freedom, nobody can give you equality or justice or anything. If you are a man, you take it." That is the jungle law! You have to seize the riches and the power if you want it.

I remember a time when I was coming up in the game and I had just started selling weight. I played the sheep role until the African I worked for discovered that I was a wolf. One day a client had failed on a payment of about $75,999 in drugs. My boss man brought the issue to me and I said I would take care of it. I kidnaped him and pistol-whipped him. The next day he paid my boss.

(5) "If your part of the battlefield is covered with thorns, you don't leave your position and go stand where the ground is good." I realized with that move he now knew I was a wolf. So instead of running off on him with money or me robbing him. I showed him I could be of use. I asked him, "Do you have anyone else that hadn't paid?" I then started to play the role of his enforcer, a wolf on a leash.

He wasn't a lion, yet more like a zebra, hiding and blending in the streets that were full of killers and robbers. Don't get me wrong, the guy had pull. He was smart, cartel-connected, spoke French and Spanish. He was intelligent as hell and a smooth guy. After that, as time went on. I now realized that with my crew behind him and me, he felt gangster. He now felt he could make threats and demands in the streets. He kept me and my crew paid in return. So, I stayed loyal and my crew stayed loyal to me.

I knew Yaya was soft. A long time ago, when I first started working for him. I played the sheep role not to scare him away. When I got to a proper position to show I was a lion, I did. I read when I was younger that...

(6) "It has always been a rule that the weak be subject to the rule of the strong that they are not deserving of power." Sometimes positions in life can change and others, you cannot change. One being who you really are. If you are born a sheep, don't try to run with the wolves. Believe me, the jungle law is concrete. I am a firm believer in it. The saying is that only the strong survive on land and at sea. Even in the sky, the biggest baddest animals prey on the smaller ones. People in today's society and in the past civilizations are no different. It's just that in today's society, people hide their rage in many different ways. In the time of kings and queens, the king did not just get the crown on blood alone. Yet by violence and cunning in other instances. They had to play their roles and position themselves. Then they were bold enough to take it. Remember never to offend the wrong person or underthink a person's ability or skill. Life is like a chess game; you will pay the price of underthinking your opponent. Move slowly and with direction. Simply put, always do your homework. Thus, baiting the hook to suit the fish.

CHAPTER 7

NEVER PUT ALL YOUR EGG'S IN ONE BASKET

"Failure is a part of the process of success." **Steve Harvey**

GAME - Lately, most of the things that we are good at now, when we first started, we were miserable at them. It's very simple how we have evolved as humans through centuries of mindless trial and error. That is how you ever learned to ride a bike, read, or even prosper at life itself. With business opportunities, it's the same you have to crawl, fall, then walk. You will fail first, that's life; it's the process we all go through. It's the power and strength in getting back up. Persistence is the determination that is what segregates the great from normal.

REVERSE - No matter what bundle you classify people in, there will always be an anomaly in life. In this instance, I am speaking on gaining business, fame, and power. For example, let's say you have one person who finally gains success and riches through years of entrepreneurial trial and error. Then you have another entrepreneur who gains equal success and riches with their first entrepreneurial endeavor. Some may say it's timing, luck, or simple economics. My opinion as a realist is it's simply destiny.

Narbeh Derhacobain said, "After losing 35 million in an IPO fail, that always kept losing in perspective and taught him to measure progress against the past."

This, to me, has always been a motivation and more of a reason to never let anyone hold me away from my fate.

STORY - I was dolo "alone" around this time, with no crew. It was just Simone and me. We now lived together in a one-bedroom apartment in College Park. I had a couple of homies that I kicked it with on some weekends. Most of them were working people. Squares were just spinning in the hamster wheel of a nine to five life. They wanted my life with the cars, clubbing and balling out on the weekdays. They hated their lives, showing out with me in the clubs on the weekends were the only times they felt free and alive. At the time, the only drug dealer that I hung out with a lot was P-roe. He was one of my big homie goodies friends. He was from College Park also. P-roe was a bonafide hustler. Hell, he even had two or three chicks prostituting for him. He was a major player and with me being younger, I also soaked up a lot of game from him. His only fault in my eyes was he liked to stay coked up. Anyone that knows me will forever tell the world that cocaine is not my thing! It just never was my style.

My dad always told me, "Playas get paid and junkies get high."

I have always remembered that, so I never did cocaine and believe me, I had plenty of opportunities. With that being said, P-roe and I kicked it sporadically. Then we went our separate ways. P-roe was still a loyal and good person and he was still my homie, right or wrong, flaws and all.

Unobstructed, I can still see myself back in those days. I had major cocaine dreams and goals. Those dreams included foreign cars, mansions, and hella diamonds. I felt like nobody was going to stop me but me. I had a crack trap at this time. In the same complex that I lived in, there was a junkie named Pops that lived there and in my absence, he ran the house. He was around 60 years old and smart as hell. Pops were cooler than penguins' feet. Pops taught me a lot about life, drugs, and women. In our late-night conversations over glasses of Hennessy, cigarettes, and blunts. He told me old stories of how they used to be so smooth in the 60s and 70s. Those were the years Pops said he used to pimp and move heroin in Baltimore, Atlanta. I used to love those conversations. To me, the 70s were extra players. It's crazy, but as I served the crack smokers. He gave me countless jewels and lessons on the game I was in. That knowledge today, I feel, was priceless. For free, those jewels he gave me took him and other hustlers years to learn, so I paid attention. I still thank him today for all the bullshit he went through for my rise in the streets.

I purchased a 1979 Caprice Coupe that I spent a lot of time and money on. It had a candy blue paint job, sound system and all. That was my hobby back then. That car kept me occupied and not hanging in the street. I was working with about a quarter kilo of cocaine and like 10 pounds of marijuana back then. Good money for a 21-year-old with no kids. I wasn't selling weight, just breaking everything down. That was good money. Still, I felt it wasn't enough! I wanted boss man money. I had to do more. First off, the money I was making took a lot of time to make. A lot of small moves and riding all over Atlanta. It was a lot of long nights posted in shady areas, even in other people's projects and hoods. I kicked it in a lot of heavy drug areas known in Atlanta as DC6 areas. I didn't give a fuck; I was trying to get my paper. There were a lot of close calls and a lot of running from the police. I felt I did it all back then, as Pops would say, "I was staying down for my crown in the streets." To me, that meant by any means necessary. Like Malcolm, I stood in the window many nights holding that ak47 tight 'for real. It was whatever back then. I was on a mission.

I had a homegirl who turned tricks for me whenever I ran into some good customers. Pops hooked me up with her. She was 26 and her name was Nikki. Pops knew her aunt and he gave me straight instructions.

He said, "Nephew Nikki is a good hoe; all she needs is hot water, and the bitch will sale like crack."

Basically, all she needed was directions and instructions. Right up until that moment, I had never dabbled in the pimp game. I was green as hell when it came to pimpin'. Nikki just needed a boss as a young nigga with vision and a hunger to win. Most importantly, she needed a money manager.

Pops told me again, "Nephew stay hard on a bitch like the mob on a snitch, young pimpin' just ride the hoe like a bumper sticker, about ya money and you will be good. Just tell her when she is fucking up!"

Strongly to this day, I feel that all a pimp is to a hoe is a manager. Nikki gave me all the game that I have to this day on prostitution and handling bitches in the street. She taught me how to check a hoe (find a fresh female) knock a hoe (take another pimps girl). She even taught me how to fuck a hoe. Believe me, it's definitely a difference. I talked to Simone, my girlfriend before I even started and to my surprise, she was kool with it. I think the thought turned her on a lot by having a man that other women sold themselves to provide for her. To me, it felt great. I felt like an all-around gangster now. I guess I never had sex with Nikki though she was like an older cousin. She showed me so much about the shady business of prostitution and how it went hand and hand with the drug game. She showed me that one pussy hair could pull a freight train. I felt that a hoe should never give that much power up for free. Nikki was my partner for real. She later brought two other females along Dream and Star. She met them while she was out handling our business. At one time, all three of them lived with Pops and to keep it one hundred, I did have sex with both of them, but not often.

Nikki told me, "Lil Bra keep ya dick in Simone, not them bitches we working and reward them with sex and more when they do good. When you do fuck them take your time, a hoe gets rushed fucked all the time."

They stayed down for a minute, all three of them living at Pops' house. His old ass loved every minute of it too. I used to laugh like hell at him getting lap dances and twerked on just for walking thru the house. I loved the fact that he had fun. I mean, what 60-year-old single man wouldn't love three sexy young females walking around his house half-naked all the time. Shit, I hope when I am that age, I have as much fun as he did. Still, back then, I had to have self-control.

Nikki's number one thing she used to always say was, "Chino, never let a female see that you love pussy!"

For me, that was extra hard to do. Still, I kept it one hundred with her, and it changed how I saw the pimp game, regular relationships, and love. I pimped for about nine months in total. That was all it took for me to realize that the pimp game wasn't for me. To be a pimp is hard work; you have to have a love and passion for conversation. A strong will, patience, and love for debating. Because you got to talk, talk, talk to a female to keep them on track and handle business. Don't get me wrong, I've always had a strong will and drive for money. Plus, I am a good talker, but I never had the patience for drama. To me, hoes asked for too damn much! You have to get their hair, nails, feet done, and outfits weekly, some daily. Then there are the drop-offs and pick-ups, keeping them fed, them always arguing, and then I was getting beef at home with Simone. The jealousy in the stable was taking its toll. I finally said fuck it right then and there; I knew I wasn't a pimp with the drama I just went through for those months. I found a whole new respect for pimps and what they do. The real players that handle the game, making a living off a woman's vagina. Real pimps that do the max in the streets, not them kidnapping, human trafficking lames, but real pimpin'. I salute you with no hesitation!

I let the game go and returned to my main job as a drug dealer. Star and Dream left like a month later to live with their mothers. Like a loyal soldier, Nikki stayed down at Pops. She renegaded the streets for a while. She still held me down when I needed a female to handle biz. I definitely did the same for her. She was an Ok girl, just caught up in the streets just like me and most of the African American youth in the inner city. Surviving in the jungle by any means necessary.

Now, this is where the story gets interesting! One day Nikki calls me and says, "Lil Bro, I got someone I want you to meet and I need you to come asap."

She also wanted some marijuana, so it definitely wouldn't be a blank trip. She knew I wouldn't turn down the money. I also thought it was a female she wanted to introduce me to. So, I went over quickly. When I arrived, it was a dark-skinned bald-headed man. I thought to myself, *"Damn, what the hell is going on over here."* I still stayed to check it out. She hugged me and introduced me, like always, as her little brother. His name was Mustafa and he was from Gambia, Africa. (This is a pivotal moment in my life because two things are about to happen. One this was my first introduction to Islam. Secondly, my first time getting a line to a major drug connection.) Mustafa says that Nikki informed him that I sold a lot of drugs around the southside and that I did good business.

I just stood there and nodded. Still on defense mode! He smiled and told me, let's talk. We walked inside the apartment and he handed me a beer. When we sat down, he told me he had access to a lot of marijuana. He said he and his brothers were looking for someone to work with on this side of town. We talked for a while. I gave him my street credentials or resume in the (legal world). He looked satisfied as he sipped his beer and we talked. He then tells me that he wants to start me out with 50 pounds on consignment. Now in my head, I was thinking, *"This nigga crazy, or this is the feds, or he just flexing in front of Nikki."* Either or I had to see what was up! I still played it kool; we smoked a couple of blunts and downed about a twelve-pack of Heineken's. At the end of the conversation, he said he had to run everything by his brother, but we will be good to go, no pressure. We exchanged numbers and I left.

That meeting stayed on my mind for the next couple of days.

Nikki called the next day and said, "Mustafa was official and that I should know by now that she wouldn't introduce us if he was some bullshit."

I asked if they were fucking and she said no, he was just kool as hell. The next week rolls around and Mustafa calls. He said he and his brother wanted to meet up with me. We both agreed on the Mexican restaurants, on Old National.

He laughed and said, "Just come eat and we talk."

I agreed and when I got there, it was Mustafa and a slim African. His name was Yaya. He was a small, frail cat. Hell, he even talked softly. Still, I could tell he paid close attention to every word I said. He watched my movements when I went to the bathroom and back to my car. I knew quickly he was the man.

He said it himself too, "I am the boss of a major crew."

He said that his crew was all African except for one American girl. He revealed that he had a Mexican Cartel Connection and he could get me anything I needed.

I laughed, "Anything?"

He smiled, "Yeah, anything marijuana, ecstasy, coke, heroin, hell even Mexican bitches." I laughed and we talked for about an hour or better.

Yaya was kool as hell. He said that if I did do business, I had to make sure of one thing. That, above all, he had to get paid no matter what. Even if I didn't get paid, he had to get paid; this was because he had to pay the cartel, no exceptions. No matter what the debt of the product laid on me at the time of my possession. I agreed, we then exchanged numbers and he said he would call me in a couple of days.

I stayed up until around 5:00 that night. It was too much in my head, cartels, Mexico, kilos, and bales of marijuana. I felt I was finally there. I felt that I was going to be rich at any moment, or the feds would hit. The next couple of days, it was the same. I couldn't sleep, it was just too much for my brain. I stayed up one night and did a little pre-planning. I did lists of people I thought I would need to make this work. I had stash houses, runners, buyers etc. I was doing my homework. "Chapter 2".

A couple of days later, I was still racking my brain. Now I was going crazy! Thinking why hadn't he called. I felt it was in an all-out loss. Then he finally called, after about two weeks. He apologized and said that he was in Mexico getting things ready. He gave me an address and told me to come over around 7:00 tonight. I agreed and was so excited that I jumped up and down. I did that so much that my Pitbull Kane wanted to tackle me. That day it felt like an eternity waiting; I just laid around and waited on 7:00. At seven, I pulled into the apartment in Riverdale and parked. The apartments were nice low-key and clean. Yaya and I talked for a minute about his trip and issues of trust, loyalty, and success in the game. I reassured him that I wanted nothing but loyalty and success for my family. I looked him in the eye and told him he could trust me, and I had his back no matter what. With a lot of time, grinding, and building of trust, Yaya would later become one of my closest friends and mentors in the big leagues I knew in the game of drug distribution and trafficking.

I found out later this game was a lot different than the street part of drug sales. We drank a couple of beers that day and then he got up and went into his room. He comes back out with a big bale of marijuana. Walking over to me, he drops it at my feet. He walks back and brings out a total of three bales. The whole time while he was doing it, he was smiling. My excitement was uncontrollable and I laughed also. He then explained that instead of giving me 50 pounds, he gave me 75. I was in shock. He said he normally didn't break the bales down, so he evened it off. He smiled and told me to cut one open and make sure it was ok. The marijuana was gangster mid-grade. I tried to keep a straight face. On the inside, I was doing backflips. I still played it kool. I hadn't had that much marijuana in a long time. Hell, when I did have it, I had to pull out a gun to get it. Now with no force, just business. This cat was giving me what years before I risked my life and freedom. Wow! I thought this is a crazy world! That moment taught me that there has to be some trust and loyalty in the game if you want to succeed.

I put the bales in three different duffel bags and put them in my car. I didn't know, but that day would be the beginning of a long ride. A ride full of stress-filled days and wild nights. A fun ride no doubt. I sold marijuana day and night for about two weeks. Which I realized later was too long for just 75 pounds. Hell, I thought I sold it fast back then.

That next week I met up with Yaya at his spot and gave him his money. To my surprise, he asked why did it take so long. I quickly responded that the streets had yet to spread the word that I had marijuana in weight. I reassured him that I felt it was all in motion, though now. I expressed to him the fact that it would be better on the next trip. I also told him I respected the fact that he never called me about his money. Most people would have driven me crazy for way less product. I knew this guy was for real and most importantly, he trusted me fully.

Yaya then said he would hit me when the new shipment came in. I said ok and left the apartment. I didn't know then, but it would be two months before I would get a call back from him. Now I have a big problem. I had to pay two rents, my house and Pops. Two car payments, mine, and Simonies, along with hella extra bills. I was stressing like hell. I felt like I had fucked up everything. Instead of investing in my core business, cocaine with my marijuana profits. Hell, even just putting the money up and stacking it. I made a grave mistake many drug dealers make when they get real money. I bought all kinds of bullshit. I bought jewelry, clothes, strip club VIP nights, club night etc. I balled out on Simone also. She got a new wardrobe and jewels. I even bought my side chick some stuff. I was blowing money fast. Like I had robbed the man. In my mind, I was thinking, *"I was going to make it right back the next trip."* I was counting my eggs before they hatched.

I hadn't heard from Yaya for two or three weeks. People were blowing my phone up for marijuana. It was crazy! Now calls were coming in for major weight. The bad thing was I didn't have any marijuana. I definitely wasn't ready for a two-month wait. Pops' house wasn't even the same. The business was slow against my better judgment. I had entrusted him with some crack to sell and to keep. Nikki was doing all she could to keep shit in order, but she stayed in and out of the house. Pops had messed up all the drugs. I couldn't blame him because he was a junkie after all. That was way too much pressure. When I finally saw Nikki, her appearance told me everything. She too was feeling the effects of my absence. She was now back snorting cocaine and was a lot smaller. She had just gotten beaten up really bad the week before and still had a black eye. She said a person named Keith did it.

I knew Keith was a real animal but still a cokehead. The fact that he beat her pissed me off. So, I told my homie from Detroit to check him for it to go to Keith's hood. Two days after that, P-roe calls. He asked me whether I could spare Keith on the strength of him. Apparently, they had done some prison time together and he was kool with him. He kept asking and vouching for him. All that Keith is a good dude shit; it was just when he got on cocaine he would go crazy. I let it slide and told my homie from

Detroit to chill.

In a crazy twist of fate, I would run into Keith in prison. He told me that he beat Nikki up because she tried to steal his money and he caught her. It's strange how the truth will still find its way out no matter what you do. My little trap was suffering and my once employees were suffering even worst. All because of my miss guidance, hell, I was suffering. I had put all my eggs in one basket. Something my father told me when I was a child to never do. Ultimately, I should have known better to do that at this point in the game. I definitely found out with that situation to never do it again. With a lot of thinking was the only way I figured I could fix this mess. I had to come up with a solution. I had to focus to fix this. So, I did I like I always have done. I got alone somewhere undisturbed and thought about the situation. A couple of hours later, I found it. I came up with a solution that would ultimately benefit one of my closest friends and me. It was simple I needed a real (Capo). An underboss, it had to first be someone I could trust fully in a world of untrustworthy people. I had lived for years with the snakes and rats. So, I understood the game. The person I picked had to have morals, values, and a work ethic like mine. After a lot of thought, I had it! My Lil homie Javon was perfect.

Javon wanted out of the square life also. He was working 40 hours a week and not making any real money. I hated to see my homie working dead-end jobs. It was killing his motivation and flair for life. He was willing, yet it was only one problem. Still, this was a plus for me. He didn't know shit about the street, drug game, marijuana, or pimping. He wanted to learn, though and most importantly, I had known him for a very long time. Number one, I could trust him. That simple fact alone is what I needed most. I began to groom Javon for my Capo position. Which later in life proved invaluable and at times disappointing, but that is still my brother no matter what we go through. Still, that is another chapter in another book of my life. All I had to do now was wait until the next marijuana shipment from Yaya came. Then I could see how my new improvements worked if this went well. I would be on my way. If not, it would all be over!

I devised a new plan in my free time. I drew up out-of-town routes and all. The distribution routes were to be with only family members and good friends. All I knew would pay me back when I dropped off marijuana and, most importantly, pay on time. I wanted to out-sell and make more money than everyone in Yaya's crew. I wanted to get the whole shipment to myself. That was my goal. In time I would reach it years later with a lot of hard work. Hell, I accomplished it, but I lost friends, family, and hella money. Still, I held it down through those storms.

Finally, the shipment arrived and Yaya called me to meet him again at his apartment. When I got there, he said he wanted to talk. We sat down at the kitchen table and he passed me a beer.

Sitting up in the chair, he said, "Chino, at the volume of weight we are moving. It takes a lot of time and money to safely get the product to Atlanta. To lose it would be a major waste of time on both sides of the border." He then sat back and sipped his beer.

I thought, *"Damn, he ain't fucking with me no more."*

He then started back, talking, "When the shipment comes. It is first-come, first-serve. Whoever moves the most gets the most."

I started to explain my ignorance and revealed that I had just started selling weight. I told him about my new plans. Explaining everything to the smallest detail. I told him how my phone was ringing off the hook.

He sat back and smiled, "Chino, calm down; everything is kool. Look, I know you just started selling weight. It's my job to know things like this. When I first met you. I saw a strong possibility of you becoming a very successful person in my organization. I picked you on how you talked respectfully and did good business. I normally would not have even called a person back that took as long as you did. I see you are motivated to handle business and you just proved me right even more with your plans. I know you will grow in this business."

I smiled and replied, "Thanks." He just smiled like he always did.

Then he stood up, "Well, there is one change, though. Instead of me giving you another 60 pounds. I am giving you 200 pounds because you gonna need it for your new plans. Also, you have three weeks this time because of shipment issues. So, build your clientele and in three weeks, you will know if it's working."

My mouth dropped and in my head, I did a flip. I thought it is definitely on! I hadn't known this man for six months, and he just gave me 200 fucking pounds! This can't be real, but believe me, it was real, and he did give me the 200 bags. With all that said, the best part of the story is this. I sold that shit in a week!

GAME - It's a basic fact of life that many things everyone thinks they know turn out to be wrong. It was quoted once that Charles Darwin said,

(1) "It's not the strongest of species that survives nor the most intelligent, but the one most responsive to change." The word diversifications definitions are assorted or various. With that said, you can

be diverse in all aspects of life. Your style of dress, places you visit, relationships, etc. The most important thing in my book to be diverse with is your investments and businesses. Thus, never put all your eggs in one basket. I have also found this to be a good thing to do in the drug game through the years. This action could also be applied to your everyday grind and hustle.

(2) "To have ultimate victory, you must be ruthless." Meaning you have to be one-track-minded when trying to meet your goals. Let nothing stop you on your rise to power.

I have always been a person that could get along with anyone or race of people. Any type of person, it didn't matter. I guess I am what you say, a people person. Well, as long as you don't disrespect me or cross me the wrong way. I am just kool. I have always felt that you would have to have that quality and diversity in friends to succeed in life. It's simple; everyone is not the same. That (spreading of eggs) diversification in my distribution was a major factor in making it successful. The fact that I branched out with different people, personalities, and places. I've dealt with killers, robbers, college students, and family men. All people that I handpicked for certain reasons. Warren Buffet once said,

(3) "Diversification is a protectant against ignorance. Most will say that diversification is not required. If a person knows what he is doing." I agree with this in the legal business and illegal. Because dealing with people in the streets or legal world, people make mistakes, and with diversification, you can gain money when a mistake happens, or the next hustle fails. I agree with Mr. Warren Buffet one hundred percent. Diversification is your cushion and in my life lessons, I have learned that

cushions are detrimental to one's survival. Everyone should feel the same. Simply because the truth behind Murphy's Law states that (if it can happen, it will.) Diversification is for self-protection in no matter what field of business you are in.

(4) "Focus on whatever ventures offer the most realistic opportunity to make the most money."

My ex-girlfriend always said I was a chameleon when it came to other people. I could always blend in with foreigners, politicians, thugs, or whatever. She used to say that I was just too friendly and got mad. I would just explain to her that I am naturally a people person. She never understood that. Still, that is who I am, besides being a student of knowledge. I have always had the motivation and drive to be rich. This is one thing I think most people dream of, yet they really don't try to gain it. They don't challenge themselves to make it. (Manifestation) So one thing I learned was to be likable. This creates business opportunities. Which lets you be diverse, spreading your eggs in different baskets

(5) "Dream big be unrealistic." This quote is basically reminding you to set high goals in life.

Think outside the box! You have to have various goals, big goals! I have owned clubs, restaurants, etc. I've possessed shares in multiple businesses. Some I didn't know anything about and others I never spent a day in. That all came from one unrealistic dream of a teenager is selling dime bags of marijuana. I've always thought that my business portfolio was diversified, but in the end, it wasn't. I found this out the hard way when I went to prison. Then I needed my finances to support me through the rough times. Like most young Black men, I didn't plan right and they failed me.

(6) "Should you find yourself in a chronically leaking boat. What do you do? The energy devoted to changing vessels is less likely to be more productive. Than energy devoted to patching leaks." Ask yourself this question, and you should want to change vessels financially other than drowning. I have studied diversification and found these jewels by losing hundreds of thousands of dollars, family, and friends. So please learn from my mistakes! My father always said,

(7) "You have to try and if you fail then so what that is the only way to learn to make it." I have always tried anything to make money and when I failed, I tried harder. I urge the readers of this book to do the same. As a caution when diversifying your business, always remember, don't stretch your resources or yourself too thin. Because ultimately, that will end with a failure. Be diversified but learn to use managers and different chess pieces to control the whole board. (life) All business is not good business.

(8) "All that glitter is not gold," So do your homework diligently on any business, legal or illegal, before you invest your time or money into it. Don't get me wrong, occasionally mistakes are inevitable. The world is just too unpredictable and unstable, and sometimes you can lose good people by making the wrong judgment. Always remember that sometimes a bluff is not a bluff but a warning. Sometimes people do mean what they say.

I remember dating Ronda (Gaga); she was from Nicaragua and had a body like a model, light brown skin, hazel eyes, and long black curly hair. I met her when Simone and I had broken up about something I honestly had done. Ronda was beautiful, smart, and elegant; her body was definitely all fire and desire! Even better, we had a connection above just sex. She was hella street too and she and her family loved me as if I was family. She gave me an ultimatum and said she would find someone else to make her number one because I was doing too much with my X Simone and other females. I thought she was bluffing; then she moved back to Miami. We talked for weeks and I honestly wanted her to come back. I told her we could even move in together. Then that same week, I had to go to Chicago; by the time I got back to Atlanta, I had a major issue. My cousin had just stolen almost a hundred thousand from me and went to Texas. I didn't tell her the situation, which was my first mistake, which led her to believe I didn't want her. The phone calls grew less mainly because I had to grind to get the money back that I had lost, which meant going out of town. I got it back right in like three weeks. I finally sat down, relaxed, and really talked to her. She told me she had met someone; again, I thought she was bluffing. I told her to give me a week which turned into a month because I had to go to Texas the next week. I called when I got back again and she told me she was pregnant. I was hurt like hell, but what could I do? She wasn't bluffing; also, she wasn't putting her eggs in one basket.

(9) "People of power, however, are undone not by the mistakes they make, but by the way they deal with them." My advice to anyone is to try everything to make your lot in life change. Never be scared to fail. If you don't try, then that only means you didn't want it. Use diversification and never put all of your eggs in one basket. (Investment). Be diverse and it will help you when trouble comes. This means you will always be able to lean on other things to keep you afloat when times get rocky. Every day

will not be sunshine; rain will surely come! Being diverse is your umbrella. Never depend on one source of income; plan or move if you want to make it to the top. Keep a backup plan! Just think, it's simple. A car comes with a spare tire, so as a man, king of this planet. You should have one too. Never put all your eggs in one basket!

MADAM C.J. WALKER

THE LAW OF PERSEVERANCE

PERSEVERANCE-*The state and quality of being insistent, obstinately, making a stand.*

Born in 1867 in Delta, Louisiana, her real name was Sarah Breedlove. Her mother and father were poor sharecroppers that worked hard to provide for her, two older brothers and sister. Sarah's parents died when Sarah was seven years old of yellow fever. Hard times led to her brother leaving and searching for work. Her older sister who was 14, was left to take care of Sarah. Her sister got married at a very young age so that she could take care of Sarah. While living with her sister, her sister's husband abused her. This horrific act forced Sarah to leave Louisiana. She moved to St. Louis, where she sold fried fish on the streets to support herself. She later got married at the young age of 15 and soon had a child. Her husband was killed shortly after, fighting for civil rights for Blacks. She was left widowed with little schooling and little money. She didn't panic; she instead used her head. Sarah always had a flair for business; she washed clothes, sold fried fish, and was a cook. Sarah held a host of other odd jobs to support her child. Flatly put, she hustled to pay the bills and took care of her young daughter.

One day while working one of her many jobs, she received a tip for a hair formula that she had been working on. She has since said that the idea for the steel comb and her hair formula came to her in a dream. With the formula in hand, she then came up with the same business formula used by companies like Avon. She got twenty thousand African American women to demonstrate and sell her hair products door to door all over the United

States. Next, she fulfilled her second lifelong dream, which was to send her daughter to college. Next, she adopted another child and started helping other families fulfill their dreams.

She did lectures all over the United States to Black women and men. She was one of the leading African American Philanthropists of her time. When the world needed her, she was there. It took her almost a lifetime to get her dream out as a successful businesswoman. She had to go through a lot of trials and tribulations. She still prevailed as the first African American female millionaire!

At the age of 40, she was once quoted as saying, "When she started mixing her hair products, most people said she was crazy and wasting her time." By the time she died in, 1919 she had made a training school for her product line and built her own factory to produce her products. She also built a marketing empire! Sarah worked with the biggest of the biggest names in her day. She worked with Booker T. Washington, Langston Hughes and a host of other Black influential activists and entertainment stars. Sarah worked tirelessly to help African Americans better their lives financially. She kept going even when faced with death, racial discrimination and a host of other roadblocks in her life. Sarah stood firm behind her dreams and her people, no matter how long it took or what it cost. She knew it would work, and it did with a little trial and error. Her legacy lives on today in hairstyles and textures all over the world. All because of a little girl that took an all-night flight from a country town in Louisiana to the end of her dreams.

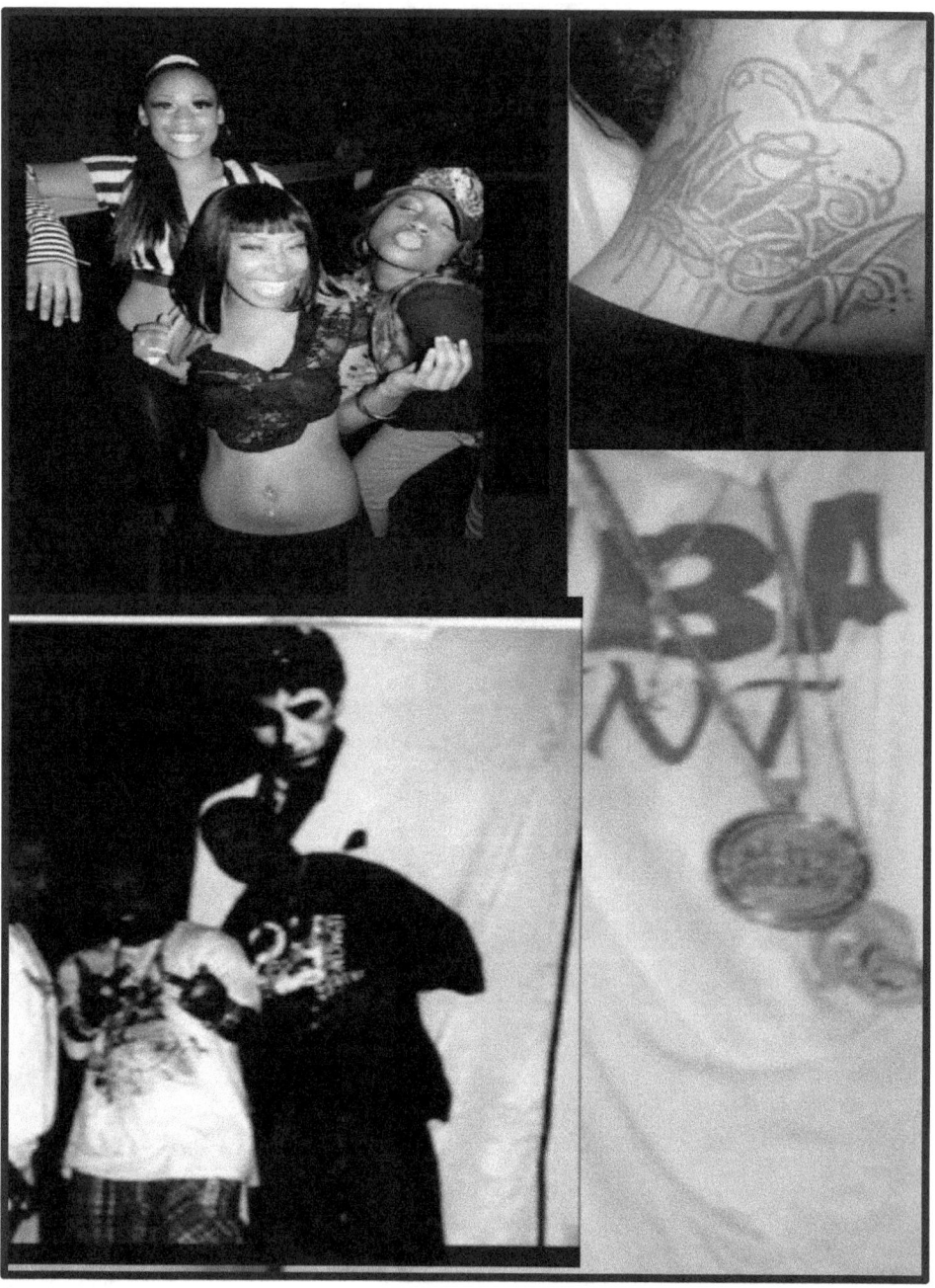

PART III

LISTEN TO YOUR INSTINCTS

"I know the ghetto people; I knew that I never left the ghetto in spirit. I never left it physically any more than I had to; I had a ghetto instinct! For instance, I could feel the tension was beyond normal in the ghetto audience and I should speak and understand the ghetto language."

Malcolm X

GAME - If your gut feeling tells you sometimes not to deal with this certain person, or not to deal with this or that mission, lick, drug deal etc., you should trust your instincts. Trust your destiny; trust the universe. Trust that there is a good reason for the feeling that you are having. Trust in your conscience; trust that it tells you good or bad paths to choose. Remember, you will always have a choice, no matter what the situation you are in. If you feel this business deal or sale will go wrong, it will be a big chance.

REVERSE - The game runs both ways in the streets, like the physical world. For example, If you have been a robber in your past, you can figure out a robbery when it is in the mist. Now let's say you are out at a grocery store and you see a person that looks suspicious and you think he is a robber. Do you risk not trusting yourself and paying the price, or do you adjust and survive? There is a high percentage that he probably is a robber. Trust your instincts because you are probably right nine times out of 10. So always remember to move and think accordingly to your instincts; they may save your life.

STEVE HARVEY

THE LAW OF PATIENCE

Patience *(noun)-The capability of enduring hardships or inconveniences without complaint.*

Steve Harvey was born on January 17, 1957, in Ohio. His mother, Eloise Vera Harvey, taught Sunday school at the local church. He grew up with something most young Black men don't have today, a stern father that installed in him how to be a man. Steve was a good kid, had good grades and was training to be a boxer. In 1985 he lived in Cuyahoga Falls, Ohio and worked as a factory worker, living check to check like the rest of the world.

As fate would have it, his first wife and kids left him mainly because Steve wanted to quit his job and follow his dreams. He felt it in his blood and soul that he was destined to be a comedian. In the beginning, Steve was making $125 a month as a low-level comedian. Most of the time, he was booking free shows. At one point, he was homeless, yet he still didn't give up, sacrificing it all. He made $25 a show to $300 a week to $700 to $25,000 a show. At the time of his Kings of Comedy tour, he made $50,000 a show. As the paychecks raised, so did his trials, tribulations, and triumphs. Still, he stayed the course.

Steve has seven children and just like his career, and he has never given up on love. Steve had two failed marriages. He got his first show called "Me and the boys," which didn't do well. Still, he kept it pushing, which led to his next job as the host of Apollo's talent show. This fit him well and the show lasted for years, making him a household name. Next was the "Steve Harvey Show," which did very well. He would later join a list of top-of-the-line comics in the "Kings of Comedy" tour, which would be the largest grossing comedy tour till this date at 58 million dollars.

Later, he would host the hit show "The Family Feud" and host the nationally syndicated radio show "The Steve Harvey Show." He also started a casual dress men's clothing line that has also done well. He is a #1 New York Times best-selling author with two books, "Act Like a Man, Think Like a Woman" and "Straight Talk No Chaser." He is an Emmy award winner and has one of the highest-rated talk shows on TV, "The Steve Harvey Show."

Steve Harvey is a person that has been through the struggle. He has never forgotten that and he has given back tremendously. Steve and his wife Marjorie have sent numerous kids to college through his Steve and Marjorie Foundation. He and his current wife, Marjorie, are deeply spiritual and in love. As it seems just like his time came to be a star, his time for love soon followed. Steve Harvey, to me, is the epitome of the law of patience. Simply because he sacrificed, suffered, and never gave up. His dedication and drive propelled him to finally live his dream as a comedian and entrepreneur. Mainly a star!

CHAPTER 8

DON'T SPIKE THE BALL

"IF YOU PRAY FOR RAIN, YOU WILL HAVE TO DEAL WITH THE MUD."

GAME - The great Napoleon Bonaparte once said, "The greatest danger occurs at the moment of victory. It is a well-known fact that in the underworld, after most major crimes in big cities involving robbery, drugs, money, etc. The FBI/detectives will go to the strip clubs, clubs, and bars because the normal human and criminal mind will party after a big score or victory. For hundreds of years army's, tribes had parties after their victories. These excessive victors' relaxation in time resulted in disaster for the once victor. In 2021, people still blindly post their victories on social media, which is gravely dangerous. Sometimes the best reply is no reply at all. Be abnormal and don't spike the ball in the ending. In his case, it might save your life.

REVERSE - By not showing a presence in the area after a victory, this action sometimes gives the competitor, or enemy time to regroup, rebuild and find a strategy to beat you or even get bold enough to attempt it. This will also make you look weak to others. Real power takes ruthlessness. Crush your enemy until there are only ashes!

STORY - At this point, business was great! Simone and I had just brought a new house in Morrow, GA. I also purchased her a new truck and a 3,000-dollar dog we named Paco. I actually got the dog to just keep her busy while I was out trafficking. I was never home, so I definitely felt she needed company. I bought myself a 1979 Moti Carlo. The car was black on black. I also had a 1979 Caprice Coupe and a new Acura to drive day-to-day. Business-wise everything was all good. Money was flowing in like an open faucet. My cousin T had just come home from prison and was eating on the streets with me. I had a small crew, but we moved big weight. From Atlanta to South Georgia and Florida. My mentor, my cousin Blackboy was still looked up for his now second prison sentence. This time I felt it was on me because I didn't get him away from the area he was grinding at. Still, business-wise, shit was Ok. It felt great letting my family get money with me. Even the niggas that I just hung around were getting money!

I was getting marijuana at this time for around $400 a pound. I then gave it to my crew on consignment for $500 a pound. Making only a $100 profit. I know you're thinking just a hundred; that's nothing. Strategically I set the price that low because of two reasons. Number one, I wanted to move it fast. Number two, I wanted to give my crew room to make money. I made up for the profit with the volume I was pushing. My crew then took the pounds and sold them for seven to $900 in certain places. I didn't care what they made as long as I got paid, and I paid Yaya.

Ever since I was young, I have always watched gangster movies and read books on gangster crews. To be honest, greed ended a lot of their reigns by them simply worrying about who makes what or who buys what.

It's crazy that even today, most of them still don't understand; as long as the money got mad as a team, then we were the ones winning.

We were moving like 700-1000 pounds a month and may be like 10-15 kilos of cocaine. Most of the cocaine I was breaking it down with a separate crew that I had on the southside in Riverdale, GA. It still was a major profit, plus I let my Lil homies eat. After all of my expenses, rental cars, trafficking fees, rent for stash houses, and bills. I was walking away with like 30 to 50 thousand a month profit. Shit was kool like I said business-wise. Emotionally I was a full-on wreak. Simone and I were growing apart. We started a lot of senseless arguing. Most of the arguments were about me being away from home all the time. She didn't understand I was holding shit down in the streets for myself and Yaya. I was either running around Atlanta, or I would be out of town. Sometimes I would be gone a month. I guess it was just way too much for her. Still, I learned a lesson with this relationship, and this goes out to all hustlers in relationships. Never think that money buys love or loyalty because it don't! It only buys comfort. A female will still want time with you. I guess it was also too many situations where I had gotten caught up cheating. Also, there were a lot of jealous females in her ear, a lot of people that she called friends. Most of them just wanted her position. I was young and thought that holding down the financial part of our lives and still spoiling her would satisfy her; I was wrong, dead wrong. She ended up doing some disloyal shit and ultimately missing her blessing. I tried to hold on to the situation, don't get me wrong, I was broken-hearted; we had been together through a lot. That was another lesson I had to learn; heartbreak is like every other problem in this world. Time heals all wounds.

My Godmother Orangie once told me when I was around 16 and going through a breakup with my then-girlfriend Adrian. "It's funny how the grass looks greener on the other side of the fence until you get in the fence and see that it was just dirt all along." As a man, I respected Simone's choices because I have been there before. Still emotionally, though, I couldn't accept it like a man. I once heard Big Mecch from BMF say, "Blood makes you relatives, but loyalty makes you family." Wise words spoken from a man I know has been through the same struggles and more. They don't tell you about the ups and downs of the game. The stressful times of this crazy game, the disloyalty in friends and family. The females, the loved ones, are crossing you out for money, drugs, all kinds of materialistic bullshit. It's a lot of kingpin or wealthy people reading this and can relate that It's heartbreaking because loyalty is priceless, and it hurts because you lose someone you loved for money or fame. I will definitely give the loyalist person I know everything! Most people don't understand how it feels to be betrayed by a loved one you actually loved. Ultimately the end result will benefit you, the one that got hurt. You grow stronger and wiser. The time and knowledge you will gain to heal are what make you a better person. I have felt that the bad days and losses were just a part of the game that ultimately made me stronger. Preparing me to deal with the heartbreak and letdowns I would face in the future when I went to prison. Still, I felt it was all part of the game that is sold, not told!

At this time, I had stopped working with Nikki; she was too wild for me. For my next steps in life, I didn't need that drama. I needed calm, clean waters if I were to sail to success. I tried, though and she just didn't fit in the crew. I wanted to help her because she really had brought it all together with the introduction to Mustafa. Still, cocaine is a hell of a drug and she couldn't see; we were going to be rich through her addiction. Pops was cooling it, though; I helped him relocate to a better apartment in Union City, GA. I checked on him and gave him money every now and then. He was an O.G and from time to time, I still needed him for advice on certain situations. I was elevating mentally also; hell, I couldn't even make myself give Pops crack anymore. He was getting old, which showed me, time doesn't stop. It was a reminder that I had to handle my business fast!

Then on March 10, 2004, God sent me a sign that showed me the true meaning of love. With the birth of my first child, my whole mentality changed; my whole world completely flipped. My outlook on the future now included two people. It was a us now and unbreakable us now. I had a choice and I chose my little girl over Simone, drugs, strippers, and loads of other vices. I acquired a new spot in a neighborhood called Hillandale in College Park, GA. We used this spot as a base. They nicknamed the house Jurassic Park because it was a jungle twenty-four seven for real. My big homie Crazy ran the spot him and my cousin T.

I also had a stash house for my bulk loads. To this day, people don't know it was my big cousin, a girl whom I won't name, that held me down. I was doing a couple of wholesale moves, maybe 10 to 20 kilos a month now. Still breaking most of it down, letting the streets eat. I had coke in Riverdale (Garden Walk Bldg.), Jonesboro (Brand on Hill), College Park (Godby Rd). These spots moved most of the coke with no problem. The business was kool, but the bullshit with Simone had scared me mentally and emotionally. I still hadn't found my way back. Then I met a girl from

Ohio named Jamie! When Jamie and I became a couple, I felt I was finally happy! I still could smell the rain coming in my dreams and thoughts, though. The business was going a little too good; I wasn't taking any losses, just 100% profit. Grandma always said she could smell the rain, and I smelled a storm.

Jamie, Ok, let me explain so that people won't get the wrong idea about our relationship. Jamie was my all, she understood what I had been through in life, love, and she had my back, right or wrong. When things went left for me, she stayed and loved me more. I actually met her a week after me and Simone spit. I know you're thinking rebound relationship, but no. I felt Jamie was God's gift to me, for giving my all to someone that betrayed me. Jamie was my angel, a person that I actually thought I would spend the rest of my life with and that love never left.

After about two years of Jamie and I being deeply in love, still with a couple of issues. The situation changed, and she and I broke up. The reason being I won't disclose because someone I really love was hurt, and the bond between us is deeper than even this. So that is the only detail I won't disclose. This was painful but mutual, and I feel we will fix it one day. The split with Jamie left me devastated and I would rather keep it between us. Every night, I started to wild out through strip clubs, bars, clubs, whatever, trying to get Jamie out of my mind. I was fucked up; I was fucking with dancers, popping ecstasy pills and smoking major marijuana trying to hide the pain. Heartbroken again and still single, I was blowing money fast! Everyone in my inner circle tried to slow me down, but I didn't listen. I was too arrogant, heartbroken, and now had a lot of trust issues. I will never regret doing what I did business-wise, but I lost a lot of good people with that decision to change it up. I still feel I did the best thing. I named this chapter don't spike the ball because that is what I got from a quote from one of my favorite people in history Napoleon Bonaparte. He once said, "The greatest danger occurs at the moment of victory." I've always felt that he said this because your guard is down when you feel you have won and are on top. You are relaxed. Most people party and celebrate, but your enemy (the loser) is regrouping, plotting, and gaining strength. This provokes new enemies to gather to attack you also. People get lazy with victory and with the game of drugs and war, laziness will get you killed or in prison for life. Hence "don't spike the ball!"

While I was partying, getting high, shopping, and kicking it with strippers, trying to hide my pain, I was slipping! Like Julius Cesar, I was blinded by my friend's smiles, not knowing it was snakes in my own grass plotting to overthrow me and bring not only me down but my whole crew. I thought I was tripping at first; then, out of the blue, when I did slow up, I began to see all the snake's moves, past and present, clearly. The sly comments on my new car, or the new paint job on my old school cars. My new Versace chain, Breitling watch or clothes. People even made comments about certain strippers I was fucking. I realized they wanted the chain, watch clothes, and actually liked the strippers. It was just too much extra shit! I couldn't understand why they were hating when I was breaking major bread. I had people try all kinds of tricks. One time someone put a GPS tracker on my car, and by fate, the only way I saw it was, I had to put air in my tire and I checked my rims. I didn't know if it was the FBI or robbers back then. I told no one but Javon and just stayed on point; either way, it was game time. People tried to rob me at least three times. Every time though, I fought fire with fire and strapped up my crew even more.

Shit was wild back then! One customer even wrote his number on all the one-hundred-dollar bills; another wrote his number on small pieces of paper and stuck it between the money. Both in hopes of getting close to my connect. I had people in my crew trying to do me like Deago in the move blow in real life. Out of loyalty, my connect would expose their plots and I handled it accordingly. He held me down when he didn't have to. People even tried to buy me out. I had offers up to $250.000 just to let them get on the direct pipeline from Mexico. I didn't budge and Yaya or the connect didn't either.

At this point, I was handling most of Yaya's shipment and all of his personal distribution clientele. He had basically given me the keys to the car. He spent most of his time in Mexico improving our shipments. I did all this work while still handling my own operation. I had formed a breakdown system with my crew on the cocaine that was doing great. Most of the time, I spent just picking up money. Javon did most of the product drops, while I did Yaya's distribution, payments to the truck driver, stash houses etc. I handled it all, working my ass off like I was at Georgia Power or something. When Yaya was in Atlanta, he stayed home, mostly watching movies or shopping with his new girlfriend, Tasha. He just was getting rich. I was the one out there in the field traveling state to state, networking, and building the distribution lines. I even traveled to Mexico to represent Yaya because he couldn't travel. I met a lot of people down there, some real killers, businessmen, and drug traffickers who would prove useful when I really needed them.

Max was one of Yaya cocaine connects; he had four in all. Max, to me, was the coolest. He reminded me of Al Pacino in the movie "Carlitos Way," yet he partied like he was Tony Montana. When Max was in town, Yaya would be busy as hell handling Max's business. For a reason, unknown Max never left the stash house once the drop landed. So, you guessed it; I ended up doing a lot of Max's running around while he stayed put. We ended up getting close, though. We would talk about family, business, and of course, drugs. To my surprise, Max was really smart and a good person at heart. He still was a high-ranking member of the cartel, with a history of violence. The crazy part is I only heard about the violence and never saw it. Other Mexicans that I dealt with told me of his temper and level of carnage. You could just tell he was a killer because he was always calm, which I admired. He ended up introducing me to a lot of Mexicans in Atlanta. For that, I was very grateful in the future because I would need every one of them. I somehow felt Max knew that and he was looking out. When shit got crazy, or we had an issue, we would all meet at Yaya's new five-bedroom house. One day Max tells Yaya and me that he has to go back to Mexico a week early to handle some serious situations about some shipments that had issues. One was in Chicago a 500-kilo shipment went missing. Another was in Macon, GA a thousand pounds went missing. That was the last straw; I guess when a thousand kilos got caught up by the police in Forest Park, GA. To me, it was fucked up because they knew Max didn't take it, but that was their way. He went to Mexico and Yaya, nor I ever heard from him again. I felt bad because I heard rumors that he possibly had got whacked, but it also showed me the level of seriousness I was playing at in the game. (R.I.P. MAX). He was a good person, maybe too good; that is why people took advantage of that. Max's situation taught me many lessons, and the biggest was this money; shit is business, not personal!

November-January that year, our cocaine shipments were on hold. Max was gone and the replacement was not working. Yaya kept calling the boss's trying to get the pipeline running smoothly. Still, it was hit and miss, and it was nothing coming for some time. From November to January 2006, a gram of cocaine or a grain of marijuana didn't get shipped from our line from the cartel. The Atlanta boss Max was gone. For those months, we did nothing! I had money saved this time, though. I had learned from the first stoppage. The idle time was killing my crew. Most of them hadn't saved anything, they were broke now and it was the holiday season. They were looking at me for answers. It was crazy! Some of them even robbed their customers while others felt I should or could pay their bills, and when we started working, they would pay me back. Now don't get me wrong, I did this family banking system with some of them and I didn't with others. I felt some just didn't deserve my help. I had a kid now and I had my own bills and responsibilities. I couldn't play around anymore. That's when the bullshit hit the fan.

In life, sometimes Allah cuts the grass for you and the snakes start to show. All I had to do was open my eyes and see them. I saw all types of problems. Everything was aired out because of their frustrations about the load. All the behind the back talk got back to me. All the dislikes of how I was handling my business and crew. Everything from the prices to the bitches I was fucking with. They complained about me not doing as much as they were or me receiving a cut of every pound or kilo. Now, I sit back and laugh about it, but I was mad as hell back then. I felt betrayed, confused, and lost. For days all types of emotional shit ran through my head. How could they be mad at me? I brought them in. I had the connection; I put the plan together, I went to all those different states and towns trafficking hundreds of pounds and cocaine. Risking my life and freedom to be able to give them a position. For years I grinded to be in a position to feed them and now they were counting my money. I couldn't believe it.

I felt sometimes I could have done it solo and kept it strictly business. I would have been able to spend three times as much money on my own on whatever I wanted! Still, I brought people in that I thought was family; I let a lot of mother fuckers eat. It was kool for them to bitch; they never saw the sleepless nights or the fights with my ex's because I was gone too much. My ex's never understood that I actually loved them; still, I had to choose my dreams. They never saw all the bullshit I had to go through to help get them to get there. They had new cars, houses, jewelry etc. Still, people will only love what you can do and see what you show them. In the present time, they never respected what they didn't see. Many of the same people that I was upset with had fucked up multiple times in the past and I let it slide. Not because I was foolish or soft. I did it simply out of love and loyalty. They lost thousands of dollars in drugs, money, etc. Now they were mad at me! I once read that if a man shows a flaw in his character, that flaw really exists. Don't try to cover up or hide people's flaws; see them as they really are and treat them as such. Instead of focusing on the stress, my crew was causing; I had bigger and more important issues. My money, my kids! I had to handle our future, which I chose to focus on.

My father taught me a thousand lessons since December 21, 1979. Still, life itself had to show me that emotions and money don't mix. Ultimately, I had to check myself.

I was spiking the ball hard, partying, getting drunk, popping ecstasy pills, and losing. I had to get straight and tighten up. I chose a higher road to travel rather than getting bitten by the snakes; I had to completely cut them out of my life. I had to get some distance from it all. I knew in my heart that they would rather see a mosquito with a Versace tuxedo walking with a foolish monkey with a platinum and diamond ring than to see me with anything in life. I had to step back, and I did. I got alone and focused and meditated about the situation. I stayed alone for hours, days at my house. I did my homework on my next moves and planned. When I came up with a solution, it was so simple I just had to evolve with my status.

Throughout history, no successful business stayed the same. I had to evolve and my crew had to evolve also, or I couldn't bring them with me. I was making too much money to be doing the things that I was doing or stressing about. I felt like I was in a fishbowl instead of the sea. Instead of them helping me, they were just watching me drowning, watching me do all the work, holding me back, and they got paid. They were laying stagnant, waiting on me to slip up and fail. Just to say I told you so, I knew he was a joke or mistake, gratifying themselves and other haters. I realized I was the boss the lion; I was born with a leadership gift, a natural coordinator. I was born in this game through blood. I was a made don in this thing of ours. I had to realize I was the hustler.

Then one morning, I thought to myself, *"I got the lines to Mexico, I got the biggest customers, I just need to tighten up, fuck them."*

I needed to go legal and I needed a new team. I reorganized my crew that night with a pen and paper. I changed my fate; I did my homework. That next day I got up early and went to the spot and got my scales, guns, drugs, everything, and I just left! It was a crazy situation, with a lot of arguing, mean mugs, and emotions. Still, like a man, I let them know that I loved them as family and as friends, and that would never change. This was business! Today we are kool, and I still got respect for those guys, but I had to go my own way. We still used to get together sometimes and go clubbing at big Atlanta events, but I felt it was fake love and I had to watch my back. I had evolved and now, it wasn't personal time; it was time for business!

GAME - I'm a firm believer that in life, goals are what keep us focused.

(1) "Goals are not only absolutely necessary to motivate us, they are essential to really keep us alive." I look back at situations now and I've realized that back then, I had lost all my composure when I was wilding out. I let my personal problems affect my business drive, which is a no-no! Mentally I felt I had won in the game. I felt that I was entitled to go fuck up a little. While I was fucking up, it cost me a lot of money and true friends. At this time, I was on a lot of ecstasies, or coming down from ecstasy, and made a lot of bad decisions. The people around me started to take advantage of the situation or crisis I was going through. For instance, my cousin J Mack stole $20,000, my cousin Bone fucked up $15,000, another cousin $30.000. I lost $160,000 in Florida on a shipment of marijuana by simply not using the same driver. A $50,000 loss in Thomasville, GA. The list could go on and on to the sum of almost

$300.000. All because I was being too friendly and too lazy to handle business.

I am not afraid to say that I was spiking the ball and losing the game by celebrating the game I had just won.

(2) "Every struggle, whether won are lost, strengthens us for the next to come. It is not good to have an easy life." My mentality had changed; I was tripping hard! One of my most loved people in history, Machiavelli, was a master at regrouping.

(3) "Prince's and republic should content themselves with victory for when they aim at more they generally lose. The use of insulting language toward an enemy arises from the insolence of victory or from the false hope of victory, which later misleads men as often in their actions as in their words. For when this false hope takes possession of the mind, it makes men go beyond their mark and causes them to sacrifice. A certain good for and uncertain better." I was doing too much; I should have been content with the situation and moved on. Ultimately building on and working with what I had. Not realizing the high of winning had me wanting more when I was in a good place in reality.

(4) "Necessity is what impales men to take action and once necessity is gone, only rot and decay are left." I had lost the necessity; I had lost the need to hustle again.

(5) "Live with your head in the lion's mouth; life is war." I had to find the hunger and grind again. Then God gave me a reset button in the birth of my first daughter. So, my advice is to look for your reset sign, your notification from God to change. He either will tell you to go harder or stop what you are doing completely. Sometimes we overlook the signs

until it is too late.

Around, 2013 a good friend of mine, Whitney, was wilding out when I was in prison. She was doing hella drugs, partying, just all-out tripping. One day I took a little time and actually talked to her. She revealed that one night she was out and somebody had drugged her and she woke up in a hotel room with three men she didn't know and her pants were halfway on. She said she jumped up and ran for the door, running out of the room. I felt so sorry for her and mad also, mad because I was in prison and couldn't help her. All I could do was talk to her; I couldn't be there to save her physically and stop her. I begged her to please stop with the wild bullshit before something bad happens. I told her to focus on her little girl and tighten up. I explained that her daughter was going to need her and the bullshit that she had just gone through was a sign for her to chill. She cried and said she wanted to stop but couldn't. I didn't hear from her for a couple of weeks, then a mutual friend Asia wrote me a letter and said that Whitney had overdosed on heroin, thinking it was molly at a party with some dudes. It hurt like hell, but I had to deal with it. I had a lot of love for that girl and genuinely wanted her to do great in life. She was smart, beautiful, and hella kool. Still, she couldn't see the forest for looking at the trees.

I knew I had to have the patience of a spider to win the game. That story and other events in my life made me denounce taking drugs altogether. My lesson in that was to be aware of the signs and blessings. Not being real superstitious or religious, I am just being real.

(6) "The moment of victory is often the moment of greatest peril. In the heat of victory, arrogance and overconfidence can push you past the

goal you had aimed for. You make more enemies than you can't defeat by going too far. Do not allow success to go to your head. There is no substitute for strategy." Set goals and go for it! I had lost my goals by achieving them too easily. I had to set new ones with better purposes. I also felt that I needed to develop an end game and stop selling drugs.

(7) "Know your enemy." I wasn't being me, so I realized I was my enemy. Of course, I had people inside my circle that ultimately meant me no good. Still, I let them get too close; it still was my fault. During all the drama and bullshit I was going through, I then started to feel the clock was definitely ticking on my run in the streets. The storm was approaching! I could feel it in my dream and thoughts. All I could think of was I definitely couldn't do this drug shit forever!

CHAPTER 9

SLOW MONEY IS BETTER THAN NO MONEY

Panic-*derives from the Greek God pan, who ruled the woods and fields. He stirred up mysterious sounds causing chaos and continuous fear.*

<u>GAME</u> - To be a great football quarterback, you have to be calm when most people wouldn't. Just imagine having a 6'8, 400 lb. giant trying to tackle you. To prevail, you have to be calm and not panic. Be focused to see the field and all the players for a pass or handoff. Always remember that life is the same way. Imagine all of your troubles attacking you and you don't panic. Success relies only on your ability to stay calm, focused, and kool under pressure. Then you will surely find an excellent outlet and ultimately make the play, eventually winning the game!

<u>REVERSE</u> - You should always remember that excessive calmness is a curse. To be too calm and not fear your coming threats can hurt you. Symbolically you're still the Quarterback and you hold on to the ball too long. Then all of a sudden, you get sacked. Resulting in a loss. Meaning if you are holding on to your issues too long, you may fumble and lose money or get sacked and go to jail. So, know when to move on certain situations.

STORY - One day I was having a conversation with my best friend Javon, the same one that took over the situation with Nikki a long time ago. I had groomed Javon for this very position showing him all I knew about the drug game. He had now proven himself as a loyal friend and business partner. Even when the fire in my life started, Javon stayed, sometimes not as close. Still, he stayed in my corner when a lot of people left. I realized that only a few would put out the fires in your life, risking their own life. Risking their money, family, and everything just to stand by your side. Through the fire! That's still another story in this book.

On this day, we had a deep conversation about legal business; we talked about the future of the operation. We discussed getting a barbershop, carwash, restaurant, club, and a host of other entrepreneurial investments. We ended up choosing the music business. Now mind you, if I knew what I know today about business and starting a business, I would have chosen anything except the music business. My experience investing in the music industry and putting out artists is the reason. It's similar to rolling the dice. As a new entrepreneur, a dice roll is not what we needed; we needed a sure thing. Still, life itself is like a chess game and you cannot undo your moves; you only have to learn from them, so my advice is to find a sure thing first.

First off, I want you to understand I didn't pick music because I wanted to be a rapper, but because I loved it. Hands down, I can put my little cousins against many rappers and they definitely would shine. I come from music; my Grandmother Sadie Williams was a singer/songwriter. She was said to have written the famous song "I'll be home for Christmas." My father was a DJ at WTUF, so music was in my life a lot.

My little cousins had superstar aspirations and talent, so I chose the music business. I wanted to be the next Russell Simmons, Jay-Z, or Jay Prince. I knew I could do it if I just set my mind to it. I felt it was my destiny and with God's help, I was going to make it. At this time, I had just met Kristie, who is now my son's mom. I spent a lot of time with her; Simone and Jamie had left me scared. I felt like they were doing their own thing and it was over. I was broken-hearted and had a lot of trust issues. Still, the game can't be on you like a T-shirt. It got to be in ya chest, like your heart. Don't get me wrong; I was fucked up.

I definitely wasn't looking for a family or love, but they both found me as destiny would have it. I was 27 years old; I had a million in cash buried, a new mansion in Lithonia, GA, a brand-new foreign car, and a fleet of other cars. I could have bought a Lamborghini or Ferrari, but my team felt the FBI would definitely come. Instead, I spent money on my family, team, and friends. This made me feel better than any car would have ever felt. In all, I was feeling good about life. I had so much money I was starting to spend crazy. Like $20,000 a month on clothes, Gucci, LV, Prada, you name it; we had it. We both had $230,000 or better new jewelry. James and I added up how much we both spent on bullshit that day. Painstakingly at that moment, we both realized that we were both tripping. Me a lot more than him for two reasons, one, I was the boss and as a boss, I was supposed to have been leading by example. Two, I knew the repercussions of my failure to handle the business, death, or prison. That day we both agreed that we had to go legit! Not just for ourselves but essentially for the future of our families. I will never forget that day as long as I live because that day we came up with NBA Records.

N.B.A (National Block Association) It was like a hustlers conglomerate. That same year we balled so hard on the southside of Atlanta the people in the hood called us (Niggas Bout Action, Never Broke Again). They gave us all kinds of hood names. This was in late 2000, way before the young rapper from Baton Rouge. Even now, I want him to know it's all love and the original N.B.A bosses respect his stamp. Still, without knowing how to market a label, we would just show up and show out. We would go wherever we wanted, sometimes out of state, spending thousands in clubs, bars, and strip clubs.

Were ever we wanted 50 to a hundred people on that same BMF shit. Mine you, I had never run a legal business, only a crime syndicate. I felt it was similar, not knowing I needed major help, legal help. I needed a partner and front man, but I didn't trust anyone. I thought about it for almost a week, and I had only one person in this world. I loved that and loved me enough and trusted, so I approached my brother Shannon with the deal of a lifetime. I offered him 25% of the company. He had to quit his job and commit all the way. Just as I would give it my all-in time and money, I would pay half of his bills, plus a little extra. He agreed after we worked out his money; I felt I was set now. I had my CEO! Next, I invited my brother's best and childhood friend into this thing of ours; his name was Marcos. I first met him when I was 14 years old. He attended college with my brother and was a close family friend. He had a college degree and would prove useful in many ways. I trusted Marcos, but he was nowhere to be found when the fire started. I spent 10 years in prison before I would hear from him. This is a person that I paid his rent, car notes, brought toys for his kid's birthdays, let him wear my jewelry, feed etc. I guess greed and lust are stronger than loyalty and love these days. I learned that life in beads loyalty in some people and jealousy in others. Still again, that's another story.

We employed 20 people on paperwork at NBA records on a day-to-day basis. There were 15 artists signed to the label. I had rappers, singers, and producers. My cousin T was the manager in the studio, and my cousin Bone was the security. I also employed a couple of other people out of my fading drug organization to help. It felt good to give them legal jobs, especially when they excelled and learned them. Javon's little brothers Tony and Lil Mat also held some major positions. We all worked hard back then; there were a lot of long days and nights. We spent a lot of time on the road. It felt good, though, because I wasn't trafficking drugs; I was trapping music. We gave out thousands of T-shirts, CDs, flyers, posters etc. Also, I could tell my family felt good about me doing something positive. I saw it in their smiles and movements. I finally felt that everyone was getting the picture and that this street shit was ending. I employed an accountant, business lawyer, publicist, and a marketing firm.

We did shows three nights a week, going to all the hot spots in Atlanta. Throwbacks, The Ritz Insomnia, all the spots on the southside. Shout out to My Homies Fresh, Big Mike (Bucalino), Chris, Dez, Crazy, Lil B, Lulu and R.I.P to my homies Puerto Rican Jonny and Troup. We balled at club Dream, Essos Velvet room, Primetime, The Compound, Fever Havana, Taboo Mariachi, Red Train etc. You name it; we balled out there. I spent thousands of dollars on my team daily. We would show up 70 people deep in NBA ENT T-shirts on that boss shit. All the strip clubs loved us; they would host special nights just for us. We would throw money all night;

they would need trash bags when they got to the stage. Back then, I had so much fun.

I admitted when I was doing all this blindly; I felt I was doing good marketing; I was very wrong. Unlike when I entered the drug game, I had no music game mentor. I had no legal business guide, so I did what I thought was marketing. I had no business plan; I felt that being around, spending money like the rappers, partying, and paying DJs and radio people would get me a record deal. I was wrong and thanks to my southside homie Big Wayne who gave me a couple of million dollars in the game. My other homie Mr. Derick Grooms and his brother Mr. College Park (DJ Smurf), started to help me get my business straight. They showed me how to promote properly and to make alliances. I couldn't believe it. In those days, I was actually marketing very wrong, ass-backward if you would ask my opinion. I was bullshitting; I had a little girl now and she was my only child; I had to reboot myself.

I would reset mentally by spending time with my little princess on the weekends. Nobody ever understood that those times with her put all the bullshit I was going through in perspective. Without her even talking to me, she motivated me more than any conversation I could have had with anyone. It kept me in the realization that I was a father first. She was my little piece of light in a sea of darkness. I had to get a break from the drug game! When I started the record label, that was my exit. Don't get me wrong, my crew still made moves, but it was all done on their own. I was on vacation; I explained to the cartel that I couldn't be involved with the drug business right now, especially when I was out promoting the label, definitely with what I was doing in the club's spending money. I definitely didn't want to draw the attention of the FBI. That was something they nor I wanted. The label would be time-consuming and I honestly didn't have time for drugs; we couldn't afford any mistakes. We both agreed that it was best to give a time limit and things would be kool. I think they were mad, but how could you be mad when I made them millions and never had a late payment. Even when I took losses, they never did.

When I was grinding, I went to a lot of states selling drugs, maybe 20 different cities getting money. I wanted to go to more spots now doing shows with my artist. I funded two mini-tours; we went to Houston, TX, Austin, TX, Jackson MIS, Tallahassee, FL, Then in Georgia, we hit Albany, Columbus, Macon, Augusta, Savannah, Valdosta, Thomasville and many more cities. That was probably one of the best times of my life and my crews. I had a lot of fun and made a lot of friends, met a lot of stars that supported my movement. I thought about my good memories all the time when I was in prison. I still would have traded it all to see my kids grow up. Those years I missed were priceless and that's being real.

Things were going good everybody was working hard; I felt like we were finally on our way. After about six months into the music business, my accountant called and said he had a business opportunity. He said that he knew of a person that wanted to sell a nightclub for a good price. He told me that the guy wanted $100.000 for the club and everything in it. I talked to a couple of people about it, and some said to do it, and some said don't do it. My father's advice was to just be aware that running a nightclub wouldn't be easy. He knew this because he had once owned a club before I was born. I thought about the proposal for a couple of days and called my brother and simply said, "Let's do it." Just like that, I became a club owner. That Friday, James named the club Over the Edge. It was located on Edgewood and Auburn Ave downtown Atlanta.

I loved owning the club but soon realized it was a lot of work. We did renovations and everything. I hired promoters and all, one of the promoters I hired was the infamous T White. The same one Young Jeezy raped about on his song "Lost Souls." He was just a local club promoter but still a bright person. I have the utmost respect for him and we did good business. I also hired a publicist to help get the word out. Marcos and Javon were put in charge of the club; they were the club's managers. This move left me, my brother T, and Bone in charge of the record label.

As fate would have it, a few weeks into running, both business fatigues started to set in. I showed major signs that I was stressed and my crew was also. Everyone now had two or three jobs, some working overtime. Some may say I have a spontaneous approach to my business marketing and tactics. Still, I have always had a method to the madness. I was always making plans the whole time I was having fun. It's just that life doesn't always go how you plan it. My plan was simple, let the club's profits pay for the studio and record label expenses just until I got a major record label deal. Which we had already gotten small offers, but as a group, executively and collectively, we decided the offers were not what we needed. We finally signed a deal with Bungalow Universal for my youngest group, Halftime; they were from Chicago.

We also signed my gangster rap group BDC (BEAT DOWN CLIQUE); they were from Riverdale, GA. I signed a group from College Park G.A Solice. They got a deal a year later through Interscope, which we did jointly with College Park records. They dropped a hit single

(THROWEND OFF) with a feature from Trill Lee from Houston, TX. We had a video on BET, MTV and VHI. The song was played nationally on the radio. We enjoyed the success, but it was short-lived. My returns on my music investment were minimal and I was starting to feel the effects financially. I spent almost $500.000 on the record label with marketing promotions and two tours. I did this all out of my pocket. I probably got back less than $100.000 in royalties and show money. I was exhausted physically now for real. I had like $360.000 in my personal money left, which was nothing compared to the millions I had initially set aside. I didn't want to call back to Mexico to tell my drug connection that I was almost broke and ready to start back. I felt I had to make it work; I felt like I had failed like I was a disappointment.

Around this time, I remember having a conversation with my dad about my situation and his advice was to try to do something different. He then mentioned real estate and how the housing market was down right now and houses were cheap. He also explained that the money would be a lot different if I did do this. It was slower than the money I was accustomed to making. He also expressed how he hated that I even sold drugs, but it was my life, my choice. He also expressed how he respected that I was also trying to get out of the drug game. He explained that real estate was legal and dependable. Another associate and I went in on a deal together for a trial run, and it worked out well. Again, that was a chess move I wish I could have redone and put more effort into it. I would have spent the $500.000 on real estate than a label.

I look back on it now and realize that I would have made a million or two off that investment in a year or two. Then I would have never started back selling drugs; ultimately, I would have never gone to prison, where I am now writing this book. Still, I believe everything happens for a reason. This book may one day divert youth from the streets or a life of crime. So, if my sacrifice, pain, and mistakes would serve as a deterrent, then that is kool with me. I have always believed in destiny and I felt that it was just that which brought me to prison. That same destiny is now bringing this book to your hands now.

The club was open, but it was costing me major money, around six thousand a month in security, liquor, entertainment, and other bills. I wasn't making money from the record label as I had planned. So now I had to go back to the drawing board; I had to come up with something fast! We had a big record label meeting that week. The meeting included me, my brother, Javon, and Marcos. At that meeting, my brother I argued, then me and Marcos got into a bigger argument. The topic was money; the club's money was coming up short. I explained that someone advised me that two of the female bartenders were stealing. The same two bartenders that were having sex with two of the bosses. The bosses were Marcos and Javon.

Marcos got mad that I accused him of being soft for this chick and telling him he was weak for females; the meeting got a little hot. I kinda felt if he didn't fix it, then he was down with this chick that was stealing my money. He got madder and then I got heated, so now it was on. He blamed the losses on bad promotions of T Whites company which was a lie; as I said, we did God's business. Marcos argued a couple of more issues, but I wasn't trying to hear it. More words were exchanged and I then got really mad. My frustration was because it was my money they were stealing; I felt played. I felt like they were playing games. The next minute or two turned into a blur and got wild. I last remember being taken out of the room by Bone and T.

The next day I was still hella upset. I felt tired, played, and I still wanted his blood. I called my dad because I felt kinda bad about putting my gun to Marcos's head the night before. My father was a little upset, but he also knew his son well. I have always had a temper. My father was like my consigliere (advisor). I have always respected his opinion on a lot of matters. He advised me that being emotional in business only slows down money. He said that I needed to keep a clear head. This enables the room to think of ways to make money or ways to stop yourself from losing money. He said that I needed to realize that you become part of the circus to entertain a clown. I needed to keep a clear head, I needed distance, and I needed to fix this shit fast. I ended up apologizing to Marcos a couple of days later, yet I felt our friendship was at an end. Still, instead of cutting out cancer, I let him betray me again and again; he did it for a female.

Six months later, I ended up selling the club for $80,000 and took a loss of $22,000 and another $47,000 in bills and expenses. The whole situation was a failure, but not a total loss simply because I had learned a lot from the situation. I wanted the fast club money instead of the slow real estate money that my dad had talked about. I learned that success is a journey, not a destination. If you think it's going to be easy, you will never be successful. I learned money doesn't come with an owner's manual and that slow money is better than no money.

GAME - Thomas Huxley, a philosopher in the 19th Century, compared life to a chess game and said,

(1) "If it was so, we should at least consider learning the moves and pieces." I learned to play chess while in prison and consider myself an okay player. I know you can relate to what I am about to say for those who play chess. Question? While playing chess, have you ever made a move on the chessboard or gotten a valuable piece taken from you? So, you understand that if you only had looked a little deeper, it was right there in your face. The looming danger, a threat to one of your pieces. If you could have planned your next move a little better, or you would have been in a better situation or position that you are now in. You would have never lost your queen, rook (car, money, drugs, job, relationship). Whatever it is that you lost, simply by being careful or looking deeper to see the danger around the corner.

(2) "One's work may be finished someday, but one's education, never."

The results would have been better if you had gotten the job, position, or not gotten locked up. There is a whole list of possibilities, but this is real life, and just like chess, there are no do-overs.

(3) "Space we can recover, time never." Life is just like chess; you have to study, plan, and plot your next move to be successful. Napoleon once said,

(4) "Hide your moves discreetly place your iron hands inside a velvet glove." Basically, hide your moves. I've always felt I had to hide my moves, to think to plan. Then and only then, you laid your hands inside a velvet glove to execute, so people don't see the danger coming. I learned from all my ups and downs, trials, and tribulations in this crazy world throughout life. I've always felt they were only tests and to make it, you

have to keep going and realize you simply learned another lesson. My father's advice about business was hard back then, yet simple to me now.

(4) "Being emotional in business slows down money; keep calm and keep a clear head and that enables you to think of ways to make money or ways to stop you from losing money." That quote was lifesaving to me. I had so many situations where my mind should have been on the money, or at best, the future of my business, family, and kids. I was mad and angry at a situation, and I failed in the mission.

(5) "To gain much, you have to sacrifice much." That was the main reason I was upset. I had put it all on the line every time. In my grind to the top, I learned lessons that cost me hundreds of thousands of dollars on the streets, and a couple of times, I almost lost my life. I had to serve a lot of years in prison to pay for my delinquencies on the streets. Still, I took it with a grain of salt. Ultimately, I think I am a better person, businessman, and father. I feel I am even a better partner in my relationship because the thoughts of failing or losing everything will certainly make you cherish everything more.

All things in life start and end in stages.

(6) "The great oak is born out of the acorn." We all start in life small, yet growth is what builds us; failure is what teaches us the lessons we need to continue in life. Knowledge helps you navigate through this life and learn how to deal with bad situations.

It's funny because the reverse of this law with relationships is the same. We all remember the old saying {The grass is greener on the other side.} I remember I was done dealing with my son's mom Kristie. I had enough; I was moments away from leaving Atlanta and going to Wichita,

Kansas. Squaring up and moving in with my youngest daughter's mom Latoya. The relationship with Kristie had hit a wall. I had tried my hardest to make it for my son. I was done, though, with Kristie and Atlanta mentally and emotionally in my head. I was lost, one woman was superficial and materialistic, and the other was mentally and spiritually aware of herself and the value of loyalty and family. Hell, I felt I was flashy and narcissistic enough; I didn't need a twin. I laugh at it now, but back then, I was really about to leave Atlanta and just walk away from the game, this time with Latoya. I didn't, though, because of loyalty and responsibility. I felt I couldn't leave my friends, team, and family, so I stayed. That was one of the worst mistakes of my life. I would later go to Kansas but under a different kind of pressure. I was on the run for murder in Atlanta when I finally got to Kansas. Latoya did everything for me and more.

Latoya cooked, ran errands and made sure I kept my head focused and on the situation, not stressing. Hell, she probably brought more weed that week for me to smoke than she ever did in her life. I was a wreck all the way around. I couldn't sleep, eat, or have sex hell; my mind wasn't on it. I was thinking about the situation in Atlanta, my other kids, my family, and even Kristie. How could I tell her that I was never coming back? How could I never see my son's eyes when he smiled at me with all the love in the world on his face? How could I tell Samaria I didn't try to fight the system and make it back to her? I had to do something; I had to fight. Maybe it was the loyalty, or maybe it was love. No matter how much I realized that LaToya loved me for real and had my back, I had to face it; I had to go back.

Ultimately, the loyalty I thought my team had for me wasn't as strong as mine to them. Still, with that said, I had to again live and learn.

(7) "Life has two rules! Number one, never quit! Number two, always remember rule number one! I almost went crazy running the club and record label. I learned a valuable lesson. Not to stretch myself too thin. I cannot watch everything or everyone. It's only one you, and you have to have good people around you who clearly understand that it is just business; it's nothing personal about business.

(8) "Business is the art of extracting money from another man's pocket without resorting to violence." As a criminal, I learned how to do real business without violence. A bigger lesson financially was that slow money is better than no money.

(9) "Book smarts can be gained, common sense is not at all common in people, and street smarts definitely ain't cheap smarts. It might cost you your life." So, watch your moves, remember you can get into way more trouble with a good idea than a bad one simply because you forget that the good idea needs limits.

CHAPTER 10

ROLE MODELS & CLONES

"If you got a hustlin ass boss, you got a hustling ass crew. If you got a robbin ass boss, you got a robbing ass crew." **Big Meech (BMF)**

__GAME__ - What is leadership? The term is so vague it's hard to know what it exactly means. People have given me two definitions of this word my whole life. Both of them you have probably heard also. The first is "lead by following," the second is "lead by example." Both are great advice and will make you a better leader. Psychologically if you are a leader of a team, crew, office etc., you have to have a great understanding that your personality will be soaked up, like rainwater to a plant. Your good days are great for the team and your bad days are horrible for them also. Your crew will also mimic your work ethic. The game on being a great leader is this. You have to be a good teacher first. Then when you do lead or teach, you have to do it from the standpoint of the person you are leading or teaching. You have to explain clearly and, most importantly, lead by example. If you want hard workers, start with yourself first. Remember that the mule only works as hard as the plow driver.

__REVERSE__ - Sometimes the glory, spotlight, and fame of being a leader are too much for people. They grow bold and arrogance sets in. They begin to talk to people as if they are kings and everyone else is peasant. This is dangerous and will only lead to your team, crew, or club's downfall. Treat people as you want to be treated. Do this and they will show you loyalty; if not, the team will turn on you and choose another leader.

STORY - I had just turned 28 and I was in a complete haze. I felt like my world was turning upside down. The record label was in disarray; the main group we were pushing at the time, called BDC (BEAT DOWN CLIQUE) out of Riverdale, GA, was in distress. At this time, I also felt they were our best chance at making a big music industry deal. Now all of a sudden, they were giving me a lot of extra trouble. I had just recently paid a total of $30,000 to a couple of radio promoters for their new single called (Where the Roof Go) and the results were coming in great. People were calling in from Florida, North Carolina, and Alabama for shows, but the group itself was in turmoil.

One member was ready for the music industry, he had the drive, hunger, and the swag of a rapper, but the other was going through a stage in his life where he was wilding out and really didn't believe in himself as much as everybody else. He was the group's backbone, though; he was one of the most talented artists I ever met. He could do whole songs, freestyle; he was just a natural artist, period. He also had one of the liveliest stage presence I ever saw. He started to slip badly; he missed studio sessions, shows, radio interviews, and then threw in the towel. I was very upset and in our final conversation, I had to step back and breathe. At that moment, I remembered what my father had once told me when my cousin Jamicle stole $45,000 from me. My dad's advice was simple he said, "Blood makes you relative, but loyalty makes you family." I realized that this artist was loyal at the time only to himself and his dream. That disloyalty had him blinded, so blinded that he couldn't see the bigger picture. He couldn't see me believing in him more than himself. He couldn't see me trying to help better his life.

I always felt the same about my crew, artist, and family. I stressed loyalty all the time and I constantly told them that if we were going to make it, we needed each other and that our loyalty was a bond thicker than blood; that our loyalty is what held us together. I had invested about $80,000 in this group alone and now I had only one member. I didn't know what to do, so I called Derick from Mr. College Park records to see if he had any advice. He had become a close friend and something like my music business mentor. He even stayed by my side throughout my prison sentence, which I applaud him for real. Real people do real shit and genuine loyalty and respect are precious because today really is definitely rare. On that day, Derick gave me some great advice. He laughed and said I had put too much money and faith into my artist instead of the project. The faith I understood, but the money I was puzzled.

He looked at me with a smirk and said, "I know you're wondering about the money." We both laughed.

Then he said, "I know you have to promote the artist, but you had done too much too fast."

To my surprise, he broke it down in street-level by saying, "Chino, keep in mind all artists are different and you always have to treat an artist as a person; you just meet on the street until they gain your trust; then, you can then go all-in with them."

He asked if I had just met this person on the street, would I have given him $80,000 worth of money or product on consignment.

I replied, "Some I would and some I wouldn't."

He smiled, "Really, Bra would you give anyone $80,000 worth of anything when you just meet them."

I laughed at his street knowledge and him trying to give me a picture of what he was trying to say.

I smiled and replied, "No."

He asked, "Why?"

"Because I don't know them."

He smiled and just said, "Exactly."

Then he leaned back in his chair and said, "Chino its loyalty first with anyone, before you invest in the music game. For one, he had been where I was trying to go in the music industry multiple times. Secondly, he was just a good person." He smiled and told me to go back to work and reevaluate my business plan, marketing, and crew.

The next week I had a label and crew meeting at the same time. It was a mandatory event everyone affiliated with NBA records had to attend. At that meeting, no one talked for like the first 20 minutes, but for me, I got my point across first. I showed them I was pissed and mainly disappointed. I disclosed the amount of money I had spent on the label and revealed that until the artist promotional team and the producers showed me a new drive, loyalty, and respect, I wasn't going to sponsor anyone or anything. That meant no clubbing, shopping, smoking, drinking whatever on my money and time. Everything was on pause until they showed major improvement, the only thing I was providing was studio time and even the studio time would be logged from now on out for every artist. Their faces showed me they understood there was no more playing around; I started with myself. First, I arrived at the studio at around 7:00 am instead of noon every day and I stayed until 1:00 am or later. Now mind you, I had a new girlfriend and she was not at all understanding of me being gone that much. I felt I had to handle my business first and sacrifice. If I didn't, nobody else would. I tried to explain it to her, but I feel my past reputation and a couple of crazy incidents had left a bad impression on her trust. She constantly thought I was up to something. That mind frame alone wouldn't let her see my drive and will to succeed. She only saw my wrongs and me not trying to fix our future.

Strangely my crew had the same mindset. I felt both were blinded because they hadn't seen my struggle to get her and them where we were at. They never saw me hustling crack in the apartment with Pops until 5:00 am. Grinding every night with a house full of crack smokers, or my first all-night flight with Lil Larry sleepy as hell. All these people knew was the clubs, foreign cars, jewelry, mansions, and balling out. They didn't know the grind and the hustle it took for me to get there, or better yet, the shit I had to go through to get them all there. All for them to be in a position to make their music and dreams come true.

I had to get back to where I was mentally at the beginning of my path to success. I had to get that flare for life back, and my crew did also. I soon saw a change in my crew; they started to do better and record better music. They now even treated the studio with more respect. During this time, the pressure I applied produced a diamond. The group Solace was formed. The same group that I talked about doing a deal with College Park record last chapter. It's strange how God works; we as humans can't see his moves on the chessboard we call life because they are simply too far ahead. I thought all was lost, but two strange events made magic and two people whom I both believed in made some of the best music I had heard to come out of our record label. These two talented people came together on their own after they both lost group members. They cliqued automatically and their sound was revitalizing and amazing; it was what we all needed. I felt it would get better, but it seems the devil had other plans. The Holy Koran says, "Allah gives you everything good in life and the bad that happens to you in life are all caused by your own doings."

I needed a new reason to provide; I needed that old hunger and fuel to make it to the top. I needed a new purpose to feed off, a new cause to motivate me to the end. I prayed for help, a reason, a sign, or something to keep me going, and I was given the group Solace. That same year I was tested multiple times mentally and physically with family, relationships eventually to the point I almost lost it a couple of times and said fuck it all. Little did I know that soon I would receive the reason to stop everything the game, the partying, everything and get serious about a legit lifestyle, my future, and my family. I got it all in one sign, one reason. I even wanted to leave Atlanta and start all over somewhere new and just straighten up and live life normally. This sign was the birth of my first son and his name was Jahhlive!

GAME - 50 Cent wrote in his book the "50th Law of Power," which he co-authored with the brilliant author Robert Greene that,

(1) "You can't control a large group of people on your own you will either turn into a micromanager, or a dictator, making yourself exhausted or hated, you need to develop a team of lieutenants who are infused with our ideas, aspirations and values." When I was selling weight, I was a lot of people's role models, but I was just trying to be me and be different. My artist, crew, family, friends, and even the streets copied my moves, styles, and habits.

I gave my son the middle name of Versace in 2009 because I felt like that was the sum of my lifestyle and his life to be also the glamour of the fame and I wanted him to be different just like I was. In, 2011 the song Versace by the Migos blew up in Atlanta; everyone was back on Versace. That was a reminder that I was always ahead of the crowd. I learned early in life that swagger jackers come with street fame. It's the gift and the curse.

(2) "Influence, on the other hand, is not power, it is the fate to alter another more powerful individual, or group's opinion, or action to your advantage." I needed clones, I needed my crew to have the same drive for success, hunger, and loyalty that I had, but I was still puzzled on how to do this.

(3) "The best way to find yourself is to lose yourself in the service of others." So that is what I did. I started back grinding for my family, for my future.

I remember being upset when I was in my second year in prison. I was upset because Jahhlive (Versace) was getting into many fights in school and he was just acting out badly. I first blamed myself for not being there and I began to think that he would end up being a troubled kid. Then I blamed his mother for doing the things that she was doing. Still, I never thought to blame him or scold him for his own actions and mischievousness, which was wrong because he had to learn what bad decisions would lead to.

(4) "We are all human and we have positive and negative factors, those who look for perfection in humans are going to become demoralized, frustrated, and unable to function, not realizing that

perfection does not exist within themselves." I thought back about the studio situation that day and I couldn't and didn't blame myself. I started the opposite way when I got in trouble. I blamed my brother, Marcos, Javon, my ex, hell all the way down to the groupies that just hung around. I had snapped at everyone one time or another why because I felt it was my money and they were just wasting money and, better yet, my time. Ultimately back then, I felt that I shouldn't have been working hard as everyone else. What's crazy is that day, I realized that I should have been working five times more than everyone else and 10 times less bullshitting. Why? Because it was my dream and they didn't care or see it; they now just saw the money.

(5) "Character cannot be developed in ease and quiet only through experience or trial and suffering can the soul be strengthened ambitions insures and successes achieved." I should have been going harder since day one.

The great Pimpin Ken once said,

(6) "If a pimps hoe is out of pocket, nine times out of ten, it is because of his poor ass pimpin'. In the game, they say a hoe is a reflection of her pimp, so the pimp has to set the proper example to get the proper results. If you are a lazy ass pimp who doesn't want to do shit, don't be surprised when you have some lazy ass hoes around you. If you look like a bum and don't care about your appearance or hygiene, then your hoes will most likely follow suit." A lot of people blame others when things don't go right. A successful leader takes the blame for the mistakes of the people under them and the greatness of success also.

(7) "Do not follow the path go where there is no path, to begin the

trail." I had to set the example first, then the good people and the people I needed would follow. The bullshit would fall off by themselves. Strangely that is what prison did to my life, as well as the people I really needed stayed and the bullshit fell back. Back then, though, I ultimately had to take the blame for my crew, artists etc., even all of their mistakes and downfalls after my incarceration. I felt it all was on my shoulder. Still, some I tried to talk to they now felt they had gotten too big in the game for me to listen. It's funny now, but they had to realize the hard way that they just felt big because they were standing on the shoulder of a giant!

I had to now actually inflict my plans on my people,

(8) "Avoid the unlucky and the reason is simple. Humans are extremely susceptible to the moods and emotions and even the way of thinking of those whom they spend their time with." The old saying goes, birds of a feather flock together. I believe this 100%. Javon told me one day in prison when we were on the phone that God had blessed me, but I brought the wrong people into my blessing; he was right. Even back then, I felt I needed new people around me, or I had to uplift the old people around me to change. At times it could prove very difficult to do. Remember the question at the beginning of the book about the sinking boat. Well, I felt I needed to change vessels.

(9) "Nothing pains some people more than having to think." First, I ultimately had to get my thoughts together. The quote at the being of this chapter by Big Meech was true and I didn't realize it. Your people are only a reflection of you. I was arrogant, flashy, and stayed partying, flossing, and putting on a show for the streets. That all had to change,

(10) "We like those who resemble us and are engaged in the same

pursuit; we like those who desire the same things as we do." If I wanted them to change, I had to lead by example and show my grind and dedication to our legal businesses, just as I had done with the illegal ones.

To me, the four most expensive words in the English language is "This time it's different." I had to change first, and then they would also,

(11) "As a gardener weeds out all the weeds in his garden, you have to weed out all the useless and impure thoughts, in your mind and cultivate toward perfection." I had to get rid of the thousand failures in my mind and uproot the laziness around me. I had to plant, grow, and harvest new goals and people. I was looking at my crew like they were messing up, but I was giving the wrong instructions, leadership and, more important, examples. I felt they all had the same dream and in the end, some of the dreams were to see me fail.

(12) "Never forget that when your employees share your passion and your vision, they still have to eat, their primary motivation is going to be money, that is just human nature." I learned this early in life, so I felt like it shouldn't have been envy, jealousy etc. The greatest lesson in this chapter is simple before your worker or crew changes; you have to change.

(13) "Studies show that many people stop pursuing a goal not because they are unwilling, or unable to put forth the effort, but when they put forth the effort, and the goal as promised is not there." That means to me that you have to simply reevaluate your goals sometimes. People have different goals; you have to find common goals valuable to you and your workers, then together, you all will work harder to gain success.

(14) "Power is the ability to define reality, and to make others accept

your definition as their own." Don't be afraid to show your power, be different, be a leader. A great man once said, "Crowds exhibit a docile respect for force and are slightly impressed by kindness, which is merely other than a form of weakness." Always remember that sometimes a lion has to roar to remind the jungle of who is king!

CHAPTER 11

THE FIRE

Catastrophe-*is a disaster, a finale, or a situation in which everything has gone wrong and there is no possible way out.*

<u>**GAME**</u> - Most of the time, if you step back and look at your life, the similarities are uncanny between your life and a maze. The more you stress about a way out, the harder it is to find a way out. With all the troubles and storms in life, there is always a calmness before it and peace after it's over. The decision is up to you to make the best of that time before and after by preparing and ultimately fixing your life!

<u>**REVERSE**</u> - In life, sometimes you can also over prepare for a situation, trial, or storm instead of getting out of the way. You grow bold and feel your preparation can lead you thru it. Your arrogance, in the end, will make you suffer, a greater loss. Sometimes it is better to stay on the shore than to be foolish and fish in bad weather.

STORY - The webster definition of catastrophe. {This finale, or situation in which all is lost and there is no way out.} It is sometimes livable. That decision is exactly what life gave me on March 19, 2010. Some may say what happened in my life was fate, yet I felt it was catastrophic. Why, because my world ended as I knew it. My life had been crazy since December 21, 1979, so crazy that violence at this point in my life was normal, but that day my train toward success was derailed. Again, I saw the signs just weeks before. I could smell the rain coming in my thoughts and feelings, even my dreams. It all warned me of a big storm in my life. I still ignored it and kept moving recklessly and ultimately; I paid the cost. At the time, I felt like I didn't want to do music as much as I once had. The bullshit around me, the drama, the arguing, and jealousy had stolen my drive and hope. By realizing that I had the wrong team, it had exhausted my enthusiasm and killed my vision for success.

I stopped doing my homework on a valuable subject, my future, and let my anger win. My actions showed that I stopped studying and applying my next moves to win. I was like everyone else, just going with the flow, whatever direction. I felt lost! I had just celebrated the birthday of both of my kids, Samaria and Jahhlive. What was extra special about that was Jahhlive's first birthday which sadly was the last good memory I had when I was on the streets. I was a wreck at this point. The pressure of the club, record label, other investments failing, and my relationship failing. My personal finances were also in disarray because of a couple of failed illegal investments. I had not sold drugs in a year in a half before this day. I ran everything off saved money, which was now getting low fast. I had slipped or relapsed and started back selling drugs. I bit the bullet and called back to Mexico to the cartel and returned to distributing for them. Something I promised I was done doing.

Mentally I was wreak; many crazy events had taken place before this that I should have seen. I didn't see God trying to show me and slow me down. I ignored it. I had committed the biggest sin; personally, I felt I had lied to God and started back selling drugs again and he was pissed.

On March 19, 2010, I felt his wrath for my deception. I won't get into details of that day due to legal ramifications and mainly out of respect for my victim's family. I have served my time for my actions and repented, pleaded to God for forgiveness. On that day, two people tried to rob me at gunpoint at my recording studio in College Park, GA, for 100 pounds of marijuana. It resulted in a shootout where one person was killed. Two lives were ruined that day, his and mine. My world changed in a split second. I shot multiple rounds out of an automatic rifle defending myself, yet today if I had the chance to relive it, I wouldn't have shot one round. For one reason, I took a life. I once read in prison that "A Black man who kills another back man does not realize his act is suicide, not homicide."

Only God knows I wouldn't have pulled the trigger. Instead, I should have thought about my son, daughters, family, and his family. This is what most don't do. I would have walked away with my life and him with his. True, I would have lost the marijuana, but I would have gotten it back in a matter of hours. Sometimes I feel I should have respected the pendulum of life and just gotten shot and robbed. Because I have also been on the other side of the gun throughout my life, committing these crimes just like he had been hungry, desperate, with nothing to lose and everything to gain. Trying to find myself trying to find life. Like I said in chapter five, everybody ain't gonna make it.

Some will get caught up and some will die. Only a few a small few will make it out. I have tipped the scale of justice in the streets too many times and won. I've been in situations that left blood on my hands and shoes and survived. Shots barely missed my head a couple of times. I look back on it and I know there is no way it was luck. God had a plan and we as humans know nothing of it. I lost a big part of my heart that day, something I will never get back. I've heard people talk about shot outs, murders etc., and they act like they aren't affected. Well, let me tell you realistically that you are. Any violence on your own people affects you and your community. You have to look deeper and eventually, you will see it. I tell this story not to glorify the situation but to reveal the outcome, which is a better me. I understand my faults for lying to God, killing someone and all of my other mistakes in life. Ultimately asking God for forgiveness, not greatness.

GAME - I once read something that Sun Tzu, the great warrior and philosopher, once said,

(1) "A sovereign should never launch an army out of anger and a leader should never start a war out of wrath." I feel this means that you should never judge while you are angry. Anger clouds your mind from rational thoughts. It's very hard for many people to make a rational thought while they are angry, or better yet, make a sound judgment to any problem at hand. Look at this example:

A boxer has to be calm to win a fight. He has to plan and execute an offense, create a defense, and adjust to the opposing fighter's offense. All at the same time fighting to win. My father once told me some great advice that I will forever keep close. I was in a situation at the time that was frustrating me badly. My capo Javon and I had just had a major disagreement about some legal business issues and my dad's only advice was.

(2) "Emotions lose money; if you stay calm and cool-headed, you then can figure out either a solution to save money or a way to make more money. When you get mad, you don't think and eventually, you lose." Ultimately, this is what I did and the issue between Javon and me passed.

In business, never trust a person that you love. One day, my father asked me to calm down when I had been incarcerated in the Fulton County Jail for like six months on a fresh murder charge and drug trafficking. I was tripping hard, stressing about my kid's welfare and my ex-Kristie's loyalty.

His advice was, "Son, your situation is because of your own doing and that is crazy when you could have taken the time and mentally took another route." This made me think about my actions; how would the situation have "turned out."

He laughed and asked, "Son, how many times in the six months that you have been incarcerated from your family and kids, would you have sold whatever you were selling?" I laughed because I was selling about a thousand pounds a month at the time of this issue.

His question was designed to see the answer myself to see what I could have done. I began to look at the severity of the situation. This small but valuable lesson made me think about how stupid my actions were and how dangerous anger is if simply not handled properly. What's more painful is the fact that it is very dangerous to others and yourself.

(3) "Every struggle, whether win or lost, strengthens us for the next to come. It's not good for people to have an easy life. They become weak." Anger is not the strongest emotion in my mind and life experiences; it is the weakest yet most dangerous.

Over the years, I learned so much by using my time wisely in prison. I recreated my thought process and produced a diamond during the pressure of solitude. The life away from my crew, family, and kids forced me through a lot of sleepless nights, tears, and pain. I learned the meaning of real-life and unconditional love. I learned that real family really matters; true love is not spoken but shown in your actions. Whether that person is far or near, it doesn't change. I learned that real loyalty is rarely found in people; it's rare as a four-leaf clover, so cherish it. Loyalty when you find it respect it. Remember that respect can be earned if you work hard enough for it, yet loyalty has to be given. I've had some of the closest people in my life betray me when I really needed them just a little. Some I needed just to hold me down on small stuff when I was in prison and believe me, it hurt like hell to find out your friends were only loyal to themselves. As the saying goes, the first cut is the deepest. I felt reborn after I felt some of my closest friends and families disloyalty. I felt like I could have faced whatever. I was made harder, colder, isolated, heartbroken, but still a diamond. Still, I prevailed; sometimes, I still felt mentally that all of the stress, issues, disloyalty, pain, and betrayal were just the results of the chickens coming home to roost and that was my punishment for the crimes I committed in the game.

In my heart, there was a deep crater because I had done so, so much in the streets, heinous crimes that I will never admit to or want to think about now. I felt my time clock inevitably had been punched and ultimately, the prison was calling. I accepted the pain, loss of love, family member, and special moments with my kids, so I took the pain to pay for the war crimes I had committed in these streets. My anger ultimately had cost me, my family, countless amounts of money, and too much else to mention. Still, I felt most of the things I lost were material and I felt I could one day gain them all back and more. The most important thing I lost forever was the time with my children and parents. That is something that has no price or returns with hours of prayer, life training, and a strong will to be a better person. I used the pain and anger as fuel for my rocket to greatness and my freedom as motivation to achieve more than I had in the time that I was on the streets.

(4) "Birds flying against the wind are the strongest those flying with it are the weak." The fight against this crazy world will only strengthen you, so you will excel when you go with the masses.

Figuratively speaking, I have seen hell dungeons in the Georgia State Correctional System. Thousands of wasted lives, wasting away like rotting roses. Imagine the mental shock of going from a house with a closet the size of a small apartment to a room where you sleep, eat, and use the bathroom in the same room. From the spoils of a good life to being incarcerated with people who really don't know life at all! People that have never left outside of Atlanta, let alone Georgia, people that never had hope. The helpless, the powerless the prisons were full of them, but they are called inmates. Some were so intelligent that they positively could have helped the outside world only if they had a chance. I witnessed the weak that couldn't survive inside. I saw men die for $20 cell phones; men stabbed multiple times for items you can find at any convenience store in America.

In 2011-2018 was when Smith State Prison was the worst in the state prison system for deaths and violence and the top five in the nation. God walked me through this hell daily. Now read the story "Footprint in the Sand" in the front of the book again, then you will understand why I put it in the book because I saw the footprints in the sand right beside me every step of the way during that time in Smith.

(5) "True courage is knowing how to suffer." I felt God put me there to suffer to learn to teach me and to slow my life down. That time showed me how to enjoy and cherish the things that really mattered in life because I all could end in a second. I was blinded by the lights and the speed of my life when I was on the streets; I couldn't see clearly; I was living la vida loca (the crazy life) for real.

I remember when I was on the streets watching American Gangster and in the movie, Denzel Washington's character Frank Lucus gives a valuable lesson. At the end of the movie, in the scene, his mother tells him that "Everyone will leave you" when the fire in his life starts. She said even his beautiful wife would leave him. She yelled and said that she would leave him if he went out and did what he was about to do. At first, I didn't understand it; then, it took me to go through my own fire and see the pain. To feel the hurt from friends, to know to actually now see their deception and then you have to revel in the disappointment. I took from that scene more than a lot of people would have; that scene revealed the depts of the street life. Also, it revealed that when the fire starts, everyone will run away for their own safety; your best friends, family, and spouse will try to leave and save themselves. What's funny is some will even still leave you, with their lives not even in danger; they still will run away. A very select few will stay and get burned themselves trying to put out your fire. That's the people that love you, that's the people who are loyal to you who actually love you unconditionally. Those are the people that have true hopes for you. Those are the people you need to build and start your new foundation around. These are the people that you need to rebuild with.

(6) "It is said that one cannot teach or bring another person to a level that he/she has not reached him/herself." In prison, I learned so much about myself, not just my physical strengths but my mental ones also. I learned the depths of hatred and the highs and comforts of real love from my family, kids, and friends (real friends).

I pray that by reading this book, chapter, or page, you don't have to go through what I have been through in life. The drugs, violence, and prison time just to find out who is really by your side. That is why I strongly suggest you start testing them now. It's funny because you test the people around you for fakeness with fake motives, fake catastrophes, storms, and disasters. Just to see if they will aid you or run the other way. You also have to test your anger and find the buttons, limits, and breaking points. Then work on finding ways to advertise them, ways to calm yourself in a bad situation. Prison to me felt like purgatory, where I was stuck in between Heaven and Hell. I had all of Hell's temptations around me drugs, gangs and violence and God gave me still a choice to make. A choice to do better, and I felt that is how you receive God's grace by making the right choice. So, I read countless books on self-help, history etc., trying to create a better me. I accepted the trials and pain. I realized that you have to make the right decision to get to Heaven, which symbolically to me was the outside world with my family and loved ones.

As fate would have it, no matter how hard I tried to stay focused in prison, trouble comes for you at times. I have been in multiple situations where I've gotten off the phone with my son's mother and my mental state would lead me to quickly get into arguments, fights, and disputes with other inmates and officers, some on purpose to fill the void. I was hurting inside, and the angry violence was how I was relieving the pressure and anger. Then one day, I realized that anger was the weakness and the vulnerability. I once was told that dig two graves when you set off on a path of revenge and anger. Anger had gotten me locked up and almost ruined my life; now it was here, still controlling certain situations in my life. I had to break free from it. I wanted to do better in life and make a better life for my children and me. I had to find a better way to deal with my anger before it killed me inside prison or made me kill someone else.

Trying to diminish my anger in itself was a task; I had just received a 20-year sentence for simply defending myself. I knew I was in a place where I had to now defend myself daily; I was now under pressure. I had just realized my son's mother was disloyal, a lot of my friends were disloyal, and a list of other issues made me highly upset. I prayed, meditated, and read, and then read more. This led me to find something else. Something I had lost through all the years of violence, robberies, and drug distribution. When I was in the streets, I had lost God; I had lost myself. I had stopped reading and writing down my thoughts, expressing how I felt. I had stopped believing that life was more than money and drugs. I had to get it back all of it. This led me to write this book; I had to channel this negative energy into a positive project, which led to good actions, which grew to better habits, which showed me that it is possible to change. It just takes work. It showed me that you would never know what you can accomplish until you try it. As the anger in a person changes and you find the good in life, the goodwill starts to change them and ultimately, your life will get better. Mentally I had to change if I wanted to be stronger if I had to win.

(7) "To show your frustration is to show that you have lost your power to stop events, it is helpless an action of a child who results to hysterical fits to get there way. The powerful never reveal this kind of weakness." This is a very powerful quote. So, I ask, are we children, or are we adults? Ask yourself this question but evaluate the last two times you were really angry. I know that you could have avoided it.

(8) "Never show that something has affected you, or that you are frustrated, that only show you have acknowledged the problem. Contempt is a dish that is best served cold and with affection." This is a very powerful quote also; it shows the growth of a person that handles his anger and uses it to excel. Learn to curb your anger like a baseball pitcher does a curveball off the mound. Use this method to strike out your opponents. This is far better than letting them see you get mad and you throw a tantrum like a child. They ultimately will win if you fail at this task, so don't fail, don't let them win, suppress your anger, and reuse it as fuel for your rocket to greatness.

ALLEN IVERSON

THE LAW OF BETRAYAL

BETRAYAL-*and the act of betraying, to be treacherous.*

Allen Iverson was born on June 7, 1975. His mother had him when she was just 15 years old. Allen's grandmother died when his mother was 16 and she and Allen were sent to stay with his great grandmother. Allen was named after his father, Allen Brughton, from Hartford, Connecticut. His father and mother met playing sports, so it was only right for them to have a super athletic child.

Allen was called Bubbuchuck, a nickname that stuck with him throughout life. The name was given to him by his mother, which was a combination of both his uncle's names. His mother started him in basketball at the age of five. The coach quickly saw that Allen had natural speed but disdain for discipline and learning the game. While playing basketball at the age of seven, he meets a lifelong friend Rashawn Langford. He and Allen would form a bond that would last forever. They would make a pack to get out of bad news AKA (Newport News, Virginia).

Allen went to Bethem High School, where he would meet another lifelong friend Tawana. She would soon get pregnant with their first child. In 1993 Allen was arrested for a fight in a bowling alley in Virginia; that situation would make the headlines. Allen was sentenced to five years in prison for his crime, some felt this fight would kill Allen's career in professional sports, but God had other plans. After heavy petitioning and the kindness of the then Virginia's Governor, Mr. Douglas Wilder. Allen was given a pardon in December 1993. The next year he would attend

Georgetown and according to Larry Platt, Bill Cosby, Michel Jordan, and Spike lee paid Allen's tuition to Georgetown.

Allen's Mercedes Benz was riddled with bullets in 1996 as he visited a friend at Hampton University. He was also drafted as the first overall pick in the NBA that year. He signed a multimillion-dollar deal with Reebok the next year. Allen was now smothered with money and also new problems. He boldly changed the face of the NBA and basketball players around the world. Allen rocked his tattoos and braids all the way to the bank. He played in the rookie challenge in 1997 and had a well-played rap song in 2001. Allen also won the league MVP and played in the 2001 All-Star game. In 2002, his interview and unforgettable statement "Practice" was seen worldwide as a testament to his defiance.

Allen had vices and problems like anyone else in this world. His struggles with gambling and alcohol led by many disappointments in his career and life only strengthened him. He was let down, sued, and tricked by family members and used simply because he had a good heart. Allen just wanted to make it for his people and provide a better life. Before going overseas, he played for the Philadelphia 76ers, Denver Nuggets, and the Detroit Pistons.

In 2010 the Turkish basketball team franchise Besiktas Cola signed him on. Allen divorced his long-time girlfriend in 2013; they had five children. He retired in 2003 and 2016 was inducted into the basketball hall of fame. Allen Iverson showed the world that hard work does pay off and that when the fire starts, only the strong will survive!

I met Allen in 2009 in Atlanta; we both were at the club, and he was with one of my close personal friends Troup. He and Allen were also close. I remember hearing that Troup had died in prison, and I thought about how Allen would take it. Allen Iverson, to me, is the definition of the following quote, "To fail, then you are on the right path; all the failure means is that you weren't afraid to try."

PART IV

ENVY

"You can be successful and have enemies, or unsuccessfully and have friends." **Frank Lucas** (American Gangster)

GAME - Unbeknownst to many people, success is a gift and a curse. Still, most people beg for it, but most don't know how to deal with it when it happens. For example, to some people, money itself could mean a great life, luxury, etc. On the other side of the coin, money could mean death through your vices, drugs, alcohol, women, robbery, HIV/AIDS etc.

REVERSE - If you are successful, then cause beware of that success. Because unknown to you, your style, talk, moves, dress code, attitude, everything will change with or without you knowing. Then people's attitudes and perceptions toward you will change. Friends will turn into your foes and some foes will turn into friends, so beware.

ALPHONSO CAPONE

BOSS'S LAW

BOSS-*To command in an arrogant manner.*

On January 7, 1899, Alphonso Capone was born in Brooklyn, New York. His father was a barber named Gabriele Capone; his mother Teressa was a homemaker that tended to their five children. Alphonso was a big kid and at the age of eight, he was the leader of his older brothers. He even was a part of Ralphs and Salvatores gang, the (Navy street boys) Alphonso was never totally a violent child, but when needed, he would flip the switch and transform into a ruthless person. His father tried to install in him the values of working at a young age. His father gave him a shoeshine kit at the age of twelve, which Alphonso would use to try to run his first extortion ring on the local shoeshine boys. He made them pay an extra penny just to shine shoes in his territory. Alphonso was an underworld capitalist before he even could drive.

His second gang, "The South Brooklyn Rippers," was his next step toward being an underworld boss. This was when he honed his skills, thug look, and reputation for violence. He started working for a Brooklyn mobster at the age of 16 by the name of Jonny Torrino. Alphonso would soon join the five points gang and fall under the leadership of Frankie Yale and Don Pablo Alto. They saw early on that Capone was a force to be recognized. He got the infamous scar on his face at Yales Club by a mobster named Frank Gallussio. He would rise in the mob and become a very reputed person and enforcer in Frank's gang. Alphonso then married his longtime girlfriend and had his first son Sonny.

One time during a routine pick-up of extortion money, Alphonso killed an Irishman that had heavy street ties to the Irish mob. At the request of his boss Frankie Yale and a personal promise from the Irish mob to get even and kill Capone. Frankie told him to flee to Chicago and while in Chicago, he would work for his old boss Jonny Torrio at the notorious Four Duces Club. He then would rise to power by using his unstoppable violence and cunning. Still keeping his ties to New York open, Alphonso employed the notorious killer Frank Niti, Machine Gun Jack Macqueen, and a host of others that at the snap of Alphonso's finger, they would unleash bullets anywhere.

Capone would separate the strong from the weak in Chicago. His good friend Frankie Yale would help him clean up Chicago as he then would help him get in position in New York. Capone was responsible for numerous murders, the Saint Valentine's Day massacre, the killing of the entire top brass of Chicago and the New York Irish mob. He was responsible for the manicure at the Adonis club and the taking of the docks from the Irish in Chicago. Capone organized the Italian Mafia in Chicago. Capone was the lion in the jungle and he would roar as loud and as often as he pleased and no one would challenge him. Capone was responsible for thousands of people's welfare and hundreds of murders and robberies in the same breath. Capone installed fear and respect in those he employed. Capone was a hands-on boss and a true Capi di tutti capi (Boss of all [the] bosses).

CHAPTER 12

BUILD YOUR TEAM

GENTRIFICATION-*The process of renewal and rebuilding.*

"Let no man separate what we created" **Big Meech BMF**

<u>**GAME**</u> - My uncle Solomon, a master carpenter, gave me some advice one day. The week before, I had gotten into some trouble and it was the cause of one of my closest friends. That day he gave me the summary on building a house and said it was just like building relationships. He explained that to build a house; you don't start from the roof; you start at the foundation. Then the walls and then the roof; without a strong foundation, your roof will not stand a rainstorm, tornado, or hurricane. The foundation has to be strong first. He looked me in my eyes and said, "Remember this, never build a house on sand (bullshit) because it will surely wash away in time with rain (troubles)." I remembered this conversation years later when I started to build my team in the streets. I always understood that loyalty and dedication to each other had to be our foundation.

<u>**REVERSE**</u> - Beware when building your team; always have a backup plan and an exit strategy. Because people are unpredictable and you cannot say what a person won't do. You might build a stone castle around your team and the entire time, the wolves are inside with you, ultimately trapping yourself inside your own deathtrap. Before we start this chapter, I wanted to give you an idea of how to structure your team by using different personalities. Just like you have a point guard and a center in basketball or quarterback in football, these players, I feel, are detrimental to you winning a championship (success).

1. **Consigliere**: Gives jewels, game on every subject, situations bad and good. A good person whose opinion you respect 100%.

2. **Musclue**: Tells you that you are messing up and if you don't like it, they will force you to see your mistakes.

3. **O.G**: A confidant and good listener, a person who is wrong or right you can tell your problems and they will help you without judging you. They have been through the ups and downs in life.

4. **Thinker**: Knows how to plot and execute; they move for your future and themselves. Plays life like a chessboard and knows he knows your moves ahead of time. Their main trait is being very observant and they are very detailed and evasive.

5. **God's body**: This person provides a very valuable peace in your life; they are the constant reminder that there is a higher being than you and they keep you in the realization that some things you cannot change because it is God's will. Their traits are deeply spiritual, faithful, and unequivocal.

6. **Wild Card**: They see money and opportunity in everything, a person that is needed and they are valuable risk-takers. Their traits are an adventurous spirit, opportunistic, bold, and brave.

7. **Soldier**: Does everything that you need to be done, a runner, Lil homie, or friend that you are teaching while they are putting in work. You are their O.G, their consigliere. Their traits are enthusiasm, durability and handy in every situation.

STORY - If you ask them about me, most people will tell you I have always been a strong person, not physically, mostly, but mentally through my whole life. I once was told never to judge a man on where he drinks but always judge him on how he holds it. Meaning judging people on their actions alone. I missed the streets a lot when I first got to the county jail in 2010. I felt like the great Atlas in Greek mythology, holding the pressure of the whole world on my shoulders. I stressed about my mother, father, siblings, nephews, kids, family, crew, my case, and record label.

I stressed about my X girlfriend the most; I think because I had a greater bond with her than anyone else at the time. I felt like she was more of my friend and confidant than a lover. I stressed until I couldn't stress anymore. It had gotten to the point where I was losing weight. That was around the time I met Mike; he was an older Black man that was also a Muslim. He was kinda quiet yet knowledgeable and a well-respected person in the jail. I respected him more, though, just for how he moved and carried himself. He gave me a little advice one day because he saw me just going through it mentally. He knew of my case, as well as my street accolades as a drug distributor. He said, "Yo young brother, whatever is going to happen is going to happen. All you can do is ask Allah for strength and then be prepared to deal with whatever comes your way. Still, before you can do that, you have to be real with yourself about your situation and start to strengthen yourself to fight the situation ahead. Just like a boxer has to train for a fight, you have to start now training yourself mentally to deal with the time ahead and still fight these people for your life." Mike gave me a lot of insight and knowledge about the streets, people, prisons, religion, and history. The brother was brilliant; most importantly to me, he gave me hope for my own future. He helped me prepare mentally for the situation I was facing. He used to ask me why I never ate with the younger people at the table. I would always tell him, "I would rather starve with a player than eat chicken with chumps." He thought that was hilarious.

Mike gave me books on history and business; he also gave me my first Quran, which, when I read it, gave me strength and faith in Allah. Basically, the brother gave me jewels that I needed when I really needed them. I once read that a great man shows his greatness by the way he treats little men. Mike was a great man and leader and I will forever be grateful for him giving me the strength I needed.

During my time in Fulton County Jail, I was on a rollercoaster of emotions. At times I felt I had failed everyone. I felt I had let my family, team, kids, and girlfriend down by still being involved with the streets. I was so stressed back then that I didn't realize that my crew was falling apart and they also had let me down. Instead of blaming them for their issues and faults, I involuntarily blamed myself. I felt they were the way they were because of bad teaching, or I simply put the wrong people in the position. Either way, I felt it was on me. I was the boss my actions, teachings and swag were shown in my crew. I felt that any legal or illegal organization has to be built strong by its heads. The reason is that if they have to withdraw from leadership by chance, that strength will make it run by itself. When I was incarcerated, my team ran in circles, like a chicken without a head.

My team failed me miserably; without me, they didn't keep the record label running or attempted to maintain or keep our name in the streets.

They slowly let the label die and also the drug distribution network. All the time, effort, and money put into it were all lost in time. My capo Javon tried to step up and hold it down, but his mind was not fit for that role, which resulted in one of my crew trying to rob him and being shot multiple times. The day I heard about his shooting in prison, I cried. I was so angry that I had to use a bag to breathe. I knew that it would have never happened if I had been there. He survived the situation and ultimately when we talked about it years later, he said the tragedy made him a better man. I felt that nobody cared back then because they didn't see my vision and now it was clear that they didn't have the vision for themselves to be better. The disloyalty showed in their actions; it showed in their dedication. I found myself upset after giving my all, and still, I was giving them my sanity in prison. I blame some in my crew more than I do some others; I took into account that the police were hot on us, the feds, and the homicide detectives in two states. Not to mention Atlanta narcotics and multiple snitches in their grips willing to testify. I always felt they were watching, but now I knew it was all magnified because of the murders. Every time my face or my little cousin's face was shown on the news about a murder, they talked about the record label. They said we used the studio as a legal front while we trafficked drugs and laundered the money through the club.

My little cousin Trez had gotten locked up a year before my situation for robbery-homicide. They tried to tie the record label and a couple of artists to the murder; it was all bad in my eyes. To the police, it was great news. We were crumbling and in the streets eyes; they loved it. Now I had to take a breath and step back to reevaluate my team at a very crucial moment in my life. I had to find out quickly who would stay loyal and who would not, also who to trust. It felt like all was lost, even myself lost to prison. I had to draw a mental blueprint fast. I had to rebuild; I first found and evaluated my own mistakes. That, in turn, exposed the disloyalty and other people's flaws that I didn't notice. That resulted in the self-understanding that all the time, I had people around me who were leches instead of real supporters and friends.

I remember calling one of my homies from Fulton County Jail and telling him that I had just received twenty years. He talked about how loyal he was going to be and not to worry. At the end of the conversation, I asked him to give my X girlfriend the 10 thousand dollars he owed me on a consignment of drugs. He agreed quickly, mainly because he knew how I would react if he didn't. So instead of just telling me to go fuck myself, he wasn't paying me like a man. He told my X girlfriend to meet him at the mall and never showed up. Next, he didn't pick up when I called; I was mad as hell at this lame not about the money but because he tried my gangster. This was the same person I had given hundreds of thousands of products to and helped take care of his family and kids. I made him hood rich and now, in a time that I needed him, he wouldn't have enough loyalty to hold me down on a fraction of what I did for him. I still let it go and moved on. While incarcerated, I realized this game wasn't like in the mafia or old gangster movies where your crew held each other down. No one ever went to my kids and gave them money or tried to help my kid's mothers out with their lives. Going through those times hurt, but it made me stronger knowing my haters were happy because I was down. Now they could get at all the females that wanted me or make money and act like they were really the boss. I felt the people I cared for should have taken care of me and at least stood up like men.

Going through that, I learned the limitations of kindness; like the Sufi Proverb says, by picking up the hurt bee, I got stung, and it hurt. My new perception of how a real crew or team moves was different. I believed in family, and I treated everyone as just that, but that love was false when the hard times came. Don't get me wrong; some very few will keep it one thousand. I never took care of my homies just to show off; I took care of them simply because I felt it was my duty as their family, a man, and a boss. That love loyalty got me hurt, just like in the movie Carlitos Way, the same love loyalty I had for my crew would ultimately make me pay the price. I have since forgiven the people who left me in the fire for dead or mentioned my name in my case or the streets. I've grown as a man.

My uncle used to tell me, "Nephew, a pussy can't be a man no matter how hard you try; it is what it is."

I've painstakingly moved to a better place in life and I now believe that it was all for a higher and deeper purpose. Believe me, it wasn't easy to get to this realization mentally. Still, I grew with a strong realization about life's true importance. I created a new blueprint and a new team. I realized that my old crew and team took the loss, not me; it was ultimately their fault for killing the love I had for them. I won in the end because I learned and grew through the pain that they caused and it didn't break me as they thought. The biggest win was that they didn't grow mentally. They are still the same, just older and a lot less respected without me! I guess they didn't realize that I was always telling the truth that, "I would rather starve with a player than eat chicken with a chump!"

GAME - I have the answer to an age-old question that only a person that has walked down the same fiery bloody path that I have will know to have the answer to. That age-old old question of why the caged bird sings. Ok, first off, let me say he is not singing because he is happy; let's get that out of your mind. He is singing because it gives him hope and faith that he will be free from the cage one day. He is singing because it is a way of revealing his dreams of freedom to the world. He is singing to warn the other birds of the misfortunes and pains of the cage. That is why he is singing.

That is how I felt in prison; I did my best to warn my family and friend of the misfortune of the cage. Still, I lost three family members to life sentences, my little cousin Trez, Tuck, and Shaquele, and four more cousins, Josh, Lil D, Lil Terry, and Tug, to multiple years in prison and too many homies to the grave. I had a big team on the streets and a lot of players, but ultimately I had had wrong game. They would have chosen whatever I had wanted to pursue and with my skills, we could have started a Fortune 500 company. I was a drug lord in the hood; that was my first mistake. Next, I realized a lot of the friends I had long ago had the wrong intentions, moves and motives.

(1) "He will find that as he alters his thoughts towards things and other people, things and other people will alter towards him." With that said, you have to be at your best to have good intentions and thoughts before trying to lead a team, army, business, workers, and faculty. At this time, my thoughts were a wreak, so my team's actions were a wreck. This also led to my business, legal and illegal, being a wreck. I tried to change the team focus, I even gave people different positions, but I got the same

results to no avail. I guess I was insane for attempting it again. Insane for trying to fix a broken system (broken boat) that was doomed from the start. Simply because I brought in people that had bad intentions if I only had used gentrification, "the process of renewal," I would have been Ok.

(2) "Blow yourself up like a building's demolition; instead of tearing it down, blow it up completely and rebuild anew." This is what I had to do.

I learned a long time ago that it is foolish to scold people. God made it this way; He saw fit to not evenly distribute the gift of intelligence. I had to start over. It was a critical time in my life. I needed very important parts of my team to be played, and I didn't have them. I have always had a consigliere (advisor) in my father, whom I have always trusted with my deepest secrets. I lacked a God body, O.G, wildcard, thinkers, hell, I even lacked loyal soldiers. I needed a real team at the level I was playing; I needed people who wanted me to be successful in life but wanted me to succeed. I needed people loyal to us as a team versus themselves.

(3) "The shortest and easiest way to make your fortune is to let people see clearly that it is in your best interest to promote them." I tried my best to show my team that if I made it, we made it. I brought them with me at every level I grew in the drug game. No matter how much it cost me, they balled out when I balled out. So, believe me, they saw the benefit in being in my crew and having loyalty and wanting us to win. They still couldn't see the future and chose to let other things control them instead of their loyalty.

In life, some people, no matter what you do or what they do, there is a lot in life that is sealed. They will be no more than what God planned for them. So to avoid the miserable, avoid the unlucky, troubled, lazy and people with no ambition, and people around you who want nothing in life. The motto that "Birds of a feather flock together." Stand out and be brilliant, be unrealistic, be ambitious with your goals. Surround yourself with different people, good people for different purposes. I feel you have to change your swagger, way of acting, talking to suit each member of your team because everyone is different and has good and bad qualities and faults.

(4) "To succeed in the game of power, you have to control the temperamental disposition of those around you. This presents a great danger. Most people operate in a whirlpool of emotions, constantly churning up squabbles and conflicts." There will be problems no matter who you deal with and the less you deal with bad birds, is always better. No man ever criticizes himself; learn to check yourself first.

(5) "You must change your style and your way of speaking to suit each person." Meaning you have to be ready to adapt to different levels of intellect, bravery, and ignorance. You have to be ready to adjust your emotions in any situation, legal or illegal. As a boss, the quickness of you making your final decision in every big situation will determine how far you and your team will go in life. Try to improve this skill, because it is the most valuable part of your power. People will depend on this power in handling any problem; never let them see you sweat! You have to build a team like a house with a strong foundation. First, there should be loyalty, trustworthiness, responsibility, and hardworking people. Then they should be in sync with your morals, your causes and your ambitions to succeed. Pick people you can honestly call family because this could mean riches, fame, notoriety, and great success or the flip side homelessness, starvation,

prison time or worst death. Think about the people in your life and begin to fill the positions of your team. Then you put in the time and the work.

(6) "The dictionary is the only place where success comes before work." That means you will still have to grind and put in what you want out of your life and from others. Doing the work is pivotal in any climb to success, investment, or personal relationship. What you put in, you get out. Hard work brings a profit but talking about it only leads to poverty. Don't talk about it, do it, and just remember to make it to the top; it won't be easy.

Next, you need people to motivate you. I remember one time one of my aunts, whom I definitely won't name, needed my help one day. She and her then-boyfriend had some street money that was coming into Atlanta. She needed me to pick it up and deliver it to her in north Florida; then, she needed help to deliver it to Miami. My aunt wasn't in the streets and I knew it was mainly for her man. She said she didn't have anyone she trusted, so I was the one she called. I agreed with no problem hell if I had to go to California for her, I would she was family, plus I needed a vacation. I hung up the phone and called Shandi and Laneice. First off, let me explain the dynamics of our relationship. We were a couple, but it was three of us and we all saw different people, but we were 100% committed to each other. I trusted them with my life when I had no one else to trust. Shandi was and forever will be my rock because she was tuff and street smart.

Laneice was the balance; she was calm and graceful like water together. We made fire and lots of it. We pack up, get the package and go to Florida. When my aunt sees them, she gives me a side-eye and calls me to the side. She is upset, telling me I was slipping, bringing randoms to the biz. I explained they were not random and that they actually were on my team. Which at the time was new to her because I never had females in my mix with business. At the time, I just said it, but they weren't officially in my business only because I hadn't seen their true potential. During the trip, my aunt watched the girls, as I figured. The last day she told me that she liked the girls and that from her conversations and observation, she felt they were actually down with me 110%. Hell, I felt the same, but what could they do for the team, other than tell me everything that was going on in the Southside.

We get to Miami, drop the money off and later on go out that night. During our conversation, the girls decided they wanted to handle more of my business. They elected to get me my first stash house. Shandi said they would live there and take care of the product. What's strange is Laneice brought it up. She said she felt like I needed it because I was moving too much product out of my house. To both of their disappointment, I told them I would think about it.

The whole time though, I was happy and proud that they had found their positions on their own, but I had to still think about it. We finished up the trip and went back to Atlanta and two weeks later, I was still slacking on the girl's advice. Then a situation happened that almost cost me my life. Javon and I had come home from the club like 5:00 a.m. I was awakened with Kristie at gunpoint. They took some drugs but didn't find the stash. I handled the situation with the robbery, which was a leak in my location by one of my little runners. The next day I tell Shandi, she gets hysterical; she says I need to move and I definitely need to get the stash apartment. She passed me back my blunt and got up about to walk out, and I stopped her because I saw she was upset.

She looks at me and says, "You could have gotten hurt and you sitting here like nothing happened. It doesn't matter that you got the robber. The fact is it happened and I honestly think you think that me and Laneice will not hold the shit down."

I smiled because she didn't know that I was already kicking myself in the ass for not doing it faster. That was why I had called her over there not to tell him about the situation. I told her to chill and gave her the five thousand dollars I had in my pocket for the apartment. She just smiled and shook her head, her and Lanice did hold shit down and to this day, I owe them another vacation!

(7) "Surround yourself with people who are going to lift you higher." I strongly feel that a person that wants nothing in life for themselves wants the same for you. Try to build your team with people who want something out of life. Find these qualities in each team member first and greatness will follow them and you. One of the best things you can do is fully understand the people around you.

(8) "The men who have changed the universe have never gotten there by working on leaders, but rather by moving the masses. Working on leaders is the method of intrigue and only leads to secondary results. However, working on the masses is a stroke of genius that changes the fate of the world." So, by changing the people around you, your world will also change.

(9) "Ironically, things that cost us money can be replaced. A good man or woman can experience bankruptcy but live to build another fortune.

This can be done several times. If a home burns down, it can be rebuilt, but the things we get for nothing can never be replaced." So build your team with those unreplaceable people and start now. If you feel that everybody is untrustworthy or evil, or you need good people around you, they most likely are. Trust your instincts, don't be afraid to change.

(10) "The best way to boycott is to build your own." Try this approach before you give up but start with yourself because you are the foundation.

CHAPTER 13

FLASH

"The stars position themselves to the sun, so be the sun."

Robert Greene

GAME - Gustave Lebon said, "Crowds exhibit a docile respect for force and are but slightly impressed by kindness. Which for them is scarcely other than a form of weakness." Sometimes walking in a room silently will get you targeted, be the lion and show your arrival with flair.

REVERSE - Sometimes the loud ones in the room are the weakest in the room. Be silent and strong at the right moment, or pay the price of your arrogance.

STORY - I remember when I was watching a wanting to be Tupac Shakur. I watched him in one of his interviews and he was wearing a big gold chain, ring, bracelets, and a gold diamond Bezelled Rolex watch. He stood up and had on all Versace gold and black with the black and gold Versace loafers when the interview was done. He then jumped into a white convertible Rolls Royce and pulled off. I remember thinking, *"Damn, this cat is kicking it like a soccer player! Draped up, dripped out in diamonds and Versace!"* I remember wishing like hell that one day I could feel that joy, wishing that one day that would be me in that car riding, ballin' like there was no tomorrow. I was young, yet I still had millionaire dreams of a better lifestyle.

I have been wearing a necklace with a cross since I was in like 5th grade, my mom had given it to me, but I bought my first gold chain in the 7th grade. It had a Jesus head pendant. That was the first gold chain that I paid for myself. It was the first sign of street fame or ballin' that I made to the world. I've always loved jewelry ever since I could walk or talk. My mother wore a lot of gold, so did my grandmother. She had gold chains, teeth, and bracelets. So I always felt I got the love of gold from them. They got me from south Florida. I realized I was a gold lover, just like them when I got older. When I was in high school, I wore bracelets, rings, and even had a gold nugget watch. By the time I was in the 12th grade, I had looked like an upcoming rapper or pimp. Those two professions were far from my mind. I just had their swagger and style when I was young.

The older people I was around said I always reminded them of my mother's father, Frank. He was a suave player type and he had hella finesse and style. I remember when my father stomped on and broke my gold and diamond Makavelli style cross pendant in the front yard. I was in the 10th grade; he did this simply because I wouldn't reveal how I had gotten the money to pay for it. I was so young and materialistic that I wasn't upset about the loss of money that I had hustled and risked my life for and bought the chain with. I was mad because I had lost a valuable tool in my swagger to attract girls and be a baller. A chain was a sign of manhood in the hood, and the pendant was new as hell in the streets. Even older dope boys asked where I had gotten it from at the time. I learned that nothing attracts attention more than diamonds and gold early as hell. Other than cash, They never lied when they said diamonds are a girl's best friend. By the time I was twenty-one, I would feel naked without some type of jewelry on my body. When I was 23, my mother told me at a family function in Florida, "Baby, take some of it off Chino; that's too much." I remember laughing because she said I looked like Slick Rick. I had on four chains, three bracelets, and four rings, probably a hundred thousand in jewelry. I felt like I needed it back then to be completely recognized or accepted as a made man in the streets. It's crazy, but I felt the jewelry made me who I was a boss, a baller, a hustler. I was so lost back then, and I didn't even know why!

By the time I was 26, it wasn't odd to see me rocking a hundred and fifty thousand dollars' worth of jewelry in the club. I felt like Jay-Z or Puffy. What can I say? I was doing what I thought was right. Back then, if the FBI had gotten at me, I had no way of explaining the jewelry, the cars, houses etc. I was simply a young dumb drug dealer with no sense of real business or a business plan. I wanted business people in my city and my circle to respect me.

I recall one night I went out to a club in Decatur, Georgia, called Essos. Just like most times, I had my crew with me, and that night, we played hard. I spent like 20 thousand just blowing money fast. Around 2:30, my brother told me to look over at the bar. I cautiously saw two White males with military-style aviator glasses on looking totally out of place. They should have just had a sign on that said police or detective on their head in bold letters. I quickly noticed; my brother said they had been watching us for about an hour throwing money, buying bottles, and smoking hella marijuana. Just ballin' like no tomorrow. I looked around and it was two more across the dance floor, but they were Black males. They tried harder to blend in, but I watched them watch us. I told my crew to stay doing what they were doing; I had a plan.

I called the waitress over, ordered 20 more bottles and 50 beers, and paid our bill with a big ass tip. When the bottles came, I started giving them out to everyone; the females came in groups. When the crowds got extra thick, I slid to the bathroom with my little cousin Bone. We waited for a second then walked out the front door. As we left the club, we both watched the rearview mirror in the Benz the whole ride to the southside to the studio. When we got there, I texted my brother and he said that 10 minutes after we left, the (undercover) FBI etc., were looking around. Then he said they moved to stand behind our VIP section like they didn't care now and wanted to pressure them. That night I had the whole house cleaned up and also the studio. I moved all drugs, guns, ledgers, etc.; everything was taken to a stash house. To my amazement, there were two Fulton County Police cars parked outside my subdivision the next day. They sat there all day just parked, watching the incoming and outgoing traffic.

At this time, I lived on Cascade in a gated subdivision that had only 12 houses and from my observation, I was the only drug dealer there. The rest of the residents were doctors, lawyers, and one professional football player. In my mind, I was tripping. I felt the cops were there for me and this was the end. I just knew I was about to get raided by the FBI or someone. I stayed in the window all day asking myself what in the hell are they watching and waiting on. They didn't come, but I felt the heat for the next two weeks. I knew they were watching. I also knew that I was deep in the drug game and way too deep to avoid it. After about three weeks, nothing happened. Still, I changed my movements and tried not to be out spending at clubs balling a little less.

A week later, I told my uncle Bo about it, and he laughed and said, "Nigga if it was the FBI, you have gone regardless of what you wear, or where you go, or do it's too late to stop doing whatever you doing. Hell, you might as well have more fun because the FBI only show up when they got your ass. You might as well do what you do and we will find out in a minute."

I got upset because he basically said I was fucked, yet when I thought about it, I realized he was definitely right and that I should have been low-key from the start. My father had warned me before all of this. He said I need to evolve to know better than be the shooting star instead of the sun. Meaning the shooting star only shines for a second, then it goes out. The sun shine's then goes away only to return and it has repeated this for millions of years. He advised me to stay low-key, focused, persistent, and chill with extravagance. The FBI never came, but I started to switch up my style a little by clubbing a little less, trying to stay under the radar.

This next story always reminds me of my mom because this is her favorite part of the movie American Gangster. This is the part in the movie about the coat and the front row seats that got Frank the wrong attention.

My mom would say, "Boy, you saw what that coat did to Frank Lucus; stop wearing all that stuff, son." I laughed about it now because she was on point and I wasn't.

Just like Frank Lucus, I was just having a good time. Frank was just out having fun, but he was stunting, flossing, or plainly showing off to the next man. I realized that spending 20 thousand dollars in one night and doing it all the time 56 people deep in a club was not normal. Just wearing almost a quarter million in gold and diamonds when you a street person is not normal, hell even in Atlanta. Some places it would be crazy to think of doing, especially in the hood.

I was tripping back then. I had a big sign on me, just like the FBI/ detective or whoever it was that night watching us in the club. I thought I was blending in, yet I stood too far out and the sign on my head read stupid, drug dealer. Hell, to the jack boys, it read paycheck. I was begging for the jailhouse or the robbing crew. I didn't even see it just like Frank Lucus, Big Meech, or any major street hustler; I was just caught up in the life. If you ever had money, then you understand. You get blinded by the light, as the song says. To be honest, you cannot see your mistakes or downfall approaching because of the light. Maybe the fame, money, cars, hoes, drugs or whatever has you blinded. You just can't see it because, at the present time, the bullshit is in your vision. That is your world.

Before I left the streets in, 2010 I saw a lot of errors in my movements and thoughts, from the excessive spending to the time that I should have been spending with my family and kids. I was always chasing money, chasing fame. It was too late for me, but I hope this chapter takes the blindfolds off your eyes. Maybe this story will show you not what to do; I wish I would have seen or was informed about the game. Hell, I wish somebody would have told me Big Meech and Frank Lucus don't put on the coat!

GAME - One of my favorite rap artists Pimp C from the southern rap group UGK, once said,

(1) "Our ancestors were kings and queens in Africa; that is why we love the gold and diamonds, and flashy things." Not knowing we introduced these things into the world. I totally agree with him. I feel we have been attracted to these symbols of royalty and our history because we are royalty! I feel we are supposed to have the gold and diamonds from our homeland. If you ever get a chance to read Chancellor Williams book "The Destruction of Black Civilization," you will feel the same as I do. Now don't get me wrong, I feel that there is a time and a place for everything. The place for a quarter-million in jewelry was not then. I know I feel that to do that, you have to be a person that is 100% legal in his business dealing, then you can buy a 50-thousand-dollar watch, a hundred thousand dollar chain. I mean, you have over a hundred thousand in diversified investments, mutual funds, real estate, and a legal business when I say legal.

(2) "Build real commitments to diversity in your organization. Just because they look different or dress different doesn't mean they are different." Diversification also means the people around you.

I feel you can buy a 50-thousand-dollar watch because it doesn't lose value, unlike a car or other street bullshit. I made many mistakes, and I sometimes did things the wrong way; still, I learned from my mistakes, which is also part of life. I was still selling drugs, tripping without a purpose. I didn't realize or understand I should have invested that 100 thousand dollars in a small business. Something like a cleaning service, trucking company etc., something stable. Hell, I could have gone corporate and got involved with franchises like McDonald's or Blimpies. The possibilities were endless. I didn't do the research; I just thought I was Ok as long as I legalized the money. This mistake is the same one that a lot of Black youth make when involved in illegal activities; you get complacent.

(3) "Money, others can attain power as well but superior intelligence, good looks, charm. These are qualities no one can acquire so others will enjoy them in you." Be mindful of the people that hang around you just to bask in your glow or receive good from your blessings.

I have always had a swagger and personality. All my life, I have been a very outgoing person. Still, I am humble, respectful, and a great conversationalist. I'm just a great people person; naturally, I can get along with anyone. Not just talk but have an intellectual and meaningful conversation about any subject from sports, politics, science, religion, history, art etc. I pride myself on the ability to be a chameleon. I've found that it's also been a major help in my salesmanship skills. Don't get me wrong, I used jewels, cars etc., to attract the big drug dealers to distribute my product. Still, I had the personality and conversation that made it work. Don't mistake my vanity for overconfidence because, just like every person on these planets, we all are vain to an extent.

I loved the feel of a half-pound of gold and hundreds of diamonds around my neck, shining like a street light. My wrist and pinky blinging, even in the dark. What persn on this planet wouldn't love that? Flat out, nobody wants to buy drugs, at a large scale from someone dressed like a junkie or less than them. So yes, I used drug dealer tools to attract the big fish. Still, I was aware of the dangers that came with that. It's a tricky game because you could also attract the wrong attention. I had rules to shining, though. I never wore jewelry while doing business, only at events or club nights. Also, I never wore hats or crazy clothing while trafficking. My dress code was mostly collar shirts or button-ups. I used to maybe were a watch or a small un flamboyant chain, but an event I felt like I had to shine to keep my name and my crew's name ringing. I had to keep the other distributors knowing that I was in the business and I was a boss. I never let people see me sweat; I never folded or bent when pressure from my actions came out. So, realize it's okay to shine.

I also did this to impress my crew. Men have always used money and wealth to impress and overpower each other. With that said, there will always be competition. Take, for instance, when the great JP Morgan had beef with Roosevelt over monopolies with U.S Steel; this ended when JP Morgan had to save the government by pressuring them to let him handle the financial state of depression. He pressured them by saying he would simply cash in a 12-million-dollar withdrawal from the bank. Knowing that they knew it would kill their already struggling banking system, he did this. He was the first person also in history to coin the phrase, "If you have to ask, you can't afford it." He was a flashy person, yet his flash was to blind his prey and kill them.

"People are always impressed by the superficial aspirations of things. At fitting times of the year, the prince should keep the people occupied and distracted with festivities and spectacles." I did things to the max to attract buyers also to promote loyalty and prestige to my crew. I held barbeques, parties, and events to promote music and the company as a brand in the streets. Again, there is danger in this because you can promote the wrong invites inside your crew. That was my mistake; I let an outsider in too close trying to promote the brand. I felt that money was the motive, but safety should have been the motive. At this point in my life and career, the key to getting paid in the streets is simple, stay hungry, lowkey, and stay out the way. The longer you stay out of jail and free, you will always get some money if you are ambitious and smart. Just have patience; the big money will soon come.

As a man, we do a lot of stuff for females' attention, just being honest! I have done my share of stunting for the females. It's no secret or nothing to be ashamed of because every animal on this planet shows out for the opposite sex to mate. It's in our DNA as humans. Just like Adam, the first man, we all one day will fall week for a woman.

(4) "A man needs to conquer women, actually reveals tremendous helplessness that has made suckers out of men for thousands of years. Look at the part of the most visible person, their greed, lust, their intense fear. These emotions they cannot conceal, and which they least have control, and that people cannot control, you can control for them." You have to break the rules of engagements and play on their wants, needs etc., to meet your needs. If being flashy help, then do it, but if not, sit down

until your time comes. Be responsible with your flash, don't be the shooting star that shines for a minute then goes out. Be the biggest brightest star, the sun and shine forever!

ASSATA SHAKUR

THE LAW OF DEFIANCE

Defiance *(noun)-The Disposition boldly to defy, or resist authority or the opposing force:*

Assata Shakur was born on July 16, 1947; her real name is Joanne Deborah Byron. She was the oldest of three children. Her mother and father divorced shortly after she was born. While her mother took her time to get her life back in order, Assata went to stay with her grandmother, Lulu and Frank Hill in Jamacia, New York (Queens). When she was three years old, her grandparents sold their house in Queens and moved to Wilmington, North Carolina, to a house her grandfather Frank had grown up in. Her grandparents then bought a beachfront cafe and ran a good business where Assata even got paid and had a job parking cars. In her teens, she would return to New York, to her mother in Queens. She still often visited her grandparents in the summer, where she would attend parties and park cars.

While back in New York, Assata attended Parson June High School in Queens. Assata was a wonderful student, but she was always was searching for more out of life. She ran away when she was 13 and stayed away for almost six months. She learned the horror of the streets and the good also. Assata was adaptable and mature; she got a job and an apartment. She was doing well on her own until she was out one day and saw a family member who took her back home to her mother.

When she returned home to her mother, she was now different, a lot more responsible. Her mother let her then go live with her aunt, where she would then attend a Catholic school. She ultimately changed her religion after high school. Assata attended Manhattan Community College, where she met a man and within a year, they got married. Her last name then changed to Chessimaried. She stayed married for a year, then divorced and moved to California to fight for Black people's liberation and help the African American revolution. She found the Black Panther Party in Oakland. There she learned the ins and outs of the Black Panthers and soon, she returned to New York.

While in New York, she works with Afini Shakur (Tupac's mother) in the Bronx ministry branch of the party. The deeper she got into the Black Panther Party, she started to see strange things happen to her. She often felt she was being followed and that the government tapped her phone. She was charged with bank robbery and soon was on the FBI wanted list. Assata then went on the run.

On May 2, 1973, she was shot in a traffic stop where a New Jersey state police officer was killed. She, Zayd Shakur, and Sundiata Acoli were all charged with the murder. She was wanted for bank robbery by the FBI in 1970 in 1972. Her picture was posted in the New York Daily News with a 10 thousand dollar reward. She was charged with kidnapping, a drug dealer, and a list of other charges a mile long. While in police custody, she conceived and had a daughter Kakuya, which pissed the court system off more. Assata was then the opposition and they started to treat her badly. While in the state's custody, they beat her, malnourished her, and kept her in inhuman living conditions. Her legal team took action and sued the state and won. She fought the court system tooth and nail from 1973 to 1974. She had five acquittals and three dismissals; she still was tried time after time with no evidence. Then it all changed in 1973 when she escaped and fled to Cuba, never to be seen again.

While in Cuba, she became a political refuge and it is said to still be there now. She is on the top of the females FBI's most wanted list with a two-million-dollar reward on her head. Assata went through so much to be such a brilliant mind and woman. Her drive, hunger, and defiance for a system against her and trying to hide her. She fought hard and gave her all to the cause of the revolution and will forever be irreplaceable.

CHAPTER 14

CHALLENGE THE NARRATIVE

"We'd rather go to our graves as slaves than to just stand up because we have learned that when a Black man stands up, his only reward for standing up is death." **T. Rodgers**

<u>GAME</u> - There has never been a major change in this world's history or civilization without bloodshed. Islam's notoriety came from the persecution of thousands of believers an non-believers. Christianity fame came from the persecution of Jesus and His followers suffering. Many great civilizations were formed by war, Rome, Egypt, Ethiopia, and the great powerful United States of America also with their revolutionary wars. There is no surprise to me that death demanded the lives of Malcolm X, Martin Luther King, Medger Evers, and too many more martyrs to name. They were all great people and gave great sacrifices for the changes regarding their people. With that being said, let me ask you this, would you die trying to change your family's future? Ralph Ellison once said, "It takes a deep commitment to change and an even deeper commitment to grow." I urge you to be committed to something that betters your family and grows.

<u>REVERSE</u> - With this change of power and the sacrifices of martyrs for a cause, continuing the cause has to be a number one priority. There has to be people that want the same goals as the martyr. If not, then their death, sacrifices, and works mean nothing. The Califa Abu Bakur carried on the prophet Muhammad's message, Paul and the disciples carried on Jesus's message, the Black Panthers and the NAACP had to carry on their martyrs' message for all of us to prevail. You have to learn the actual

message from the Martin's, Gandhi's, Mandelas's, and Tupac's. We have the moral responsibility to look deeper and find the ground, then build strong mental structures upon it. If not, then their deaths would be forgotten and for nothing. This reverse is unthinkable and as a part of humanity, we should all be afraid of not changing ourselves and honoring those who paved a way with their own blood.

STORY - I remember reading how to break a slave when I was incarcerated in Clayton County, GA. It was 2001, I was jailed for a probation violation. I felt like a captive, a slave myself. That single book made a big impact on my life. The book said that you break a slave the same way that you break a horse. You take the freedom out of him; you break his spirit, stripping him of his dignity. You break his train of thought, his pride, his way of movement. Then you impose your own programming on him to fit your needs, then install your fears inside him and his offspring through different tactics.

Today, what pains me about Black people in the United States is the family structure, pride, and culture, and most don't know the tribe is broken. The mentality is still warped; sometimes, I find these faults and effects in my own character and past. I remember being called a house nigga by the darker-skinned kids because of my lighter skin and good hair. I hated my darker-skinned brother before I even knew them, at times because of their walk, talk, or geographical area. All of that came from the mental restrictions of slavery's past. We have a lot of Black men in America still scared to cross the color barrier when it comes to business. Not just business with Whites, or Spanish etc., but with the Black people in your community. For fear of them gaining more than you, or being crossed, or tricked. Most Black businessmen will give another race a chance before we will a Black man. Then we have some youth cowering under the perception that the Black race is inferior. This effect is because of TV, warped historical books, and other things designed to oppress their light. When all actuality, we are better, in many ways.

My uncle, Ronnie on my mother's side, asked me when I was around 12 years old, who I was, where I came from, my culture, and my purpose as a Black man on this earth. The question left me speechless because I had no solid answers. Then he explained that the culture that I did have was bullshit, slave shit, soul food, blues, rap music, all African American bullshit, and definitely not real African culture. The real me was a descendent of kings and queens, great military leaders, that raised major civilizations out of nothing in Africa. As a youth, I didn't know that the blood that flowed through my veins was still tainted by slavery rapes and selected breeding. There was still royalty, honor, and the strong will to survive, build, lead, and conquer. He asked why don't they call American Whites, European Americans like they call us African Americans, or the Indians, Native Americans. He proceeded to give me jewels. All that night, I thought about every word that he had said and I definitely couldn't sleep. I have always remembered that day and without me knowing it has strongly tried to challenge the narrative.

As a youth, I never knew the extent of the Black American man's chains every day. The pressure from a society that looks at you from the start as a secondary human. Then as a Black man, we help the machine when we kill, poison, sell, and downgrade the most prized possession that we have. That is our brothers and, most importantly, our sisters. I have sold hundreds of kilos of cocaine in the hood, positioning thousands, maybe millions of lives. Unknowingly killing the future in my own community. Hurting my people, my race, our culture. There was no love, no pride left in me. There was only selfishness and greed, the effects of being broken. I was supposed to be the household leader, hood, community, but just like the horse, I was broken and semi-trained to hate others and live under the master's rules. The child will know only whatever you show them as a father. A drug dealer, pimp, hustler, scammer, etc. If they are there and not incarcerated bogusly or dead from the causes of the machine also. All these things add to the narrative.

In my lifetime, I've read enough books on slavery and Black History that I probably could have at least a bachelor's degree in that subject. Don't get me wrong, these are mostly my opinions, yet those opinions are based on facts. In today's time, we fear other Blacks incoherently because of betraying, robbery, snitching etc. When I was in prison, I saw how the Whites, Latinos, and Asians banded together, no matter where they were from or how they lived on the streets. They fed each other, helped out, and cared for one another as a unit.

On the other hand, I watch the Black separate themselves for the craziest reasons, gang affiliation, religion, and mainly geographical area of birth and residence. What is more baffling, I watched as they hated each other without talking to one another. That hatred was so deep that people were killed because of it. I find that very sad, but all facts.

I have a million stories in my mind that I could tell you about challenging the narrative and breaking the chains of slavery's past. The best way I can help, or better yet, we can help, will be for you and me to change our own narratives. Break our own chains first, and I feel I am doing it right now by writing this book. I am informing you my tribe, my people, on a better way to live. Also, you, the reader, are challenging the narrative by reading this book and informing yourself on a better way out. We all have a story where we were challenged by the chains of racism and history past. Some broke them and they restricted some. You have to inform yourself of the habits, traits, and deceptions of the chains to break them. To do that, you must read, learn, and inform yourself regarding the placing of this chain. You must find yourself in the past to forge a better future.

GAME - Enigmatic to most people is the actual strength of the mind.

(1) "Man is made, or unmade by himself in his armory of thoughts, he forges the weapon by which he destroys himself, or builds himself. There is really no game to give on the subject of challenging the narrative. The solution is simply the beauty of the situation. It's simple, you have to read, learn, and better inform yourself of the snares of that life. You have to find and want a better way for you and your family, descendants, community, etc. Thus, challenging the narrative of the outcome of slavery. You have to first drop the slave mentally completely. You have to learn to stop fearing the narrative and the change to come. The fear of a different route and different situations alone scares so many people from change than you can think.

(2) "This past, the Negro past of rape, fire, death, and humiliation, fear day and night. Fear as deep as the marrow of the bone. This past, this endless struggle to achieve and reveal and confirm a human identity, contains for all its horrors something very beautiful. People who cannot suffer cannot grow. They will never discover who they are." I strongly agree that we have to find out who we are first. We have been through the worst of times with slavery, mental and physical bondage. Now we have to grow and get rid of the effects and taboos of slavery's ghost.

(3) "Education is your passport to the future for tomorrow belongs to

the people who prepare for it today." This was a quote from the great El Haji, better known as Malcolm X! It's strange that people don't fear prison, jail, or the police where I am from.

(4) "If one continually surviving the worst that life can bring, one eventually ceases to be controlled by fear of what life can bring." Without that fear, we will eventually see success whenever we pursue the right path. If we as a people don't succeed, then that only means we are not trying hard enough.

(5) "Human nature is so constituted that it can't assist a helpless man, although it can pity him and even this it cannot do long. If the signs of power do not arise." So, by now, the pity from other races has been diminished because we as a people are bullshitting with our own freedom and destiny ourselves.

(6) "Stand on you on, two Black feet and fight like hell for your place in this world." In 1976, Hebert Gutman said in his book "The Black Family In Slavery and Freedom," "Slavery had weakened and destroyed the African American family, but in some small way strengthen it." I find that crazy and honorable because it shows my ancestor's strength and will to make it.

(7) "There is no cure that does not cost." John Blossomgame in 1973 said in his book "Echochlogy Herskouts" "The most remarkable aspect of the whole process of enslavement, the extent to which the American born slave was able to retain their ancestor's culture." In these crazy times, we have lost this struggle. This again showed me the fight that our people had to put up just to be African. There is no fight in today's society, that struggle shown in Malcolm, Martin, Marcus Garvey, and hundreds of

others that fought and suffered the trials and tribulations to get us where we are today. In my opinion, with all of the pain and struggle they went through, we are still blinded, at least 75%.

(8) "We all grow up with the weight of history on us all. Our ancestors dwell in the attics of our brain as they do in the sprawling chains of knowledge hidden in every cell of our body." That very DNA should propel you to do better, uplift you, your seeds, and your family.

It is said that,

(9) "Whatever the mind of man can conceive and believe it, then he can achieve it." We have to believe in ourselves first, and then others will believe in us, as well. As others begin to believe in themselves, this brings up everyone in your circle, then the community, state, etc. One of my favorite people in history, Malcolm X, believed that the African American problem was dependency. We depend on the government, its leaders, its system when it was designed from the start for us to fail and to be kept at the bottom. Everyone but us, meaning Black people have to find that fire inside us first, then challenge the narrative, then and only then will we start to live a better life for our families and us.

(10) "A man cannot ride your back unless it is bent, keep standing tall, keep climbing." I urge you to stand tall, drop the drugs, clubs, etc. and pick up more meaningful possessions like knowledge, wisdom, and better education.

(11) "There greatest weapon in the hands of the oppressor is the mind of the oppressed." Still, we as a people have to want to change and strongly pursue our goals relentlessly. The government won't help you; they will only aid in keeping you blindfolded and you making them rich. If

you keep your pockets full of coins, you will always have small change.

(12) "We have conveniently forgotten that the land we now stand on was once the possession of indigenous people who are now disproportion concentrated on reservations and reduced to alcoholism." The American Indians conformed to their wishes and you see what that got them. So, I beg you don't fold, don't bend, stand strong, and stand firm.

We as a people have to not let the traps of the oppressors trick us; we have to go to school, get educated, and better our families. It starts with the man!

(13) "There is nothing more dangerous and destructive in a household than a frustrated and oppressed Black man." It's not going to be easy to stop selling drugs, striping, clubbing, using drugs, and correcting our lives. Just remember that nothing in this world that was great was achieved easily.

(14) "The negro must remake his past to make his future." Your friends might leave you, your girlfriend, even family members might not hang around you. Because of the new, you won't fit in with the old crowd. Don't worry because new friends, girlfriends, and the family that is down for you will stay and grow.

(15) "Racism systematically verifies itself anytime the slaves can only be free by imitating his master." We must learn that we cannot copy the European ways of living. We must build our community and family structure, yet we must never forget the old days or structure and culture of our people.

We as a people have to relive that traps are set for us, the position we play in their game.

(16) "I've freed thousands of slaves; I could have freed thousands more if only they had known they were slaves." There will be doubters and naysayers that believe they are okay living in America. They are afraid of the brilliance and skills of the youth and have no reservation for supremacy. This frightens them. So instead of helping them and letting your brain and your children's brain go to waste. Water it and give it light with knowledge. Believe me, it will grow.

(17) "The blood that unites us is thicker than the water that divides us." Show your children African culture instead of European culture. Show your children something other than bullshit. I advise you to aid your husbands in the struggle and guide your children to do better to women. I want every woman that has ever dated any man and he was good to you, to try to help that brother out seriously.

In today's time, 75% of the population thinks that we are free. Why do I feel that we are given this limited freedom? It's simple to produce and provide for the masters. In today's time, we are just on a bigger plantation. To get out of this economical enslavement, all we have to do is look deeper and we will see the chains still attached through their schemes.

(18) "At a minimum, nearly 300 million Africans were murdered in that part of the MAAFA, that is more than this country's population today." The wrongful death of five to six million European Jews at the hands of their brothers doesn't compare with just one of the atrocities done to Africans in this world. King Leopold's massacre of 10 million Congolese Africans was only a starting point in the slavery game. I still sympathize with the Jewish race, but my race suffered also and we have yet to be assisted.

Today with all this pain, knowledge, and struggle in our history, we still kill each other with impunity and ease. Like it doesn't affect you or your own community and family. The little boy or girl that got shot in the drive-by could have cured cancer, aids or helped our world progress. He or she could have become a doctor that saves your dying grandmother or grandfather's life. So, I ask you to be better than your teachers and save another person from the effects of the chains of slavery.

(19) "Poor is the apprentice that does not surpass his master." Be better than the oppressor, don't oppress your own people, hating the next man is not freedom, that slavery, so be different and challenge the narrative.

JAY-Z

THE LAW OF MANIFESTATION

Manifestation *(noun)-something visible or evident that gives ground or the belief in the existence or presence of something else.*

On December 4, 1969, Shawn Cory Carter (Jay-Z) was born in New York and would later be brought home to the Marcey Projects. From the start, the odds were stacked against him. He was born into one of the worst parts of Brooklyn. Still, he thrived admits the hustle and bustle of the big apple. Jay-Z had a father that lived the street life, like most young African American males at this time. He also had a mother that loved and cared for her son. Despite the odds, Jay-Z was brilliant even at an early age. So brilliant that he taught himself how to ride a bike.

In 1980 at the age of 10, his father left home, never to return. This left Jay-Z with a burden and he knew he was in a position that most young Black men face today. He needed his father. He was now lost to teach himself how to be a man. Well, himself with the dangerous aide of the streets of New York.

Jay-Z met Jaz-O selling drugs in his projects in 1984. They soon became good friends. This relationship would gain him a deeper love for music and rap. Jay-Z attended George Washington high school. It was said that he was a smart kid, although he did not graduate. His classmates recalled Jay-Z as a quite soft-spoken person, always dressing nice. A friend named Dehaven introduced him to the drug game and he quickly excelled in it. He was now on the level of moving kilos of cocaine out of state. While still moving drugs, he traveled to London in 1988 with Jaz-O and Irv Gotti. The next year, 1989, Jay-Z received his first record deal.

Jay-Z spent the entire next year honing his rap skills while still selling drugs.

In 1994 as fate would have it, an attempt on his life was made, for reasons unknown, the gun jammed, and Jay-Z survived. That single event changed his life forever. He stopped selling drugs and got serious about music. He met Damon Dash and Karim Biggs, and they formed Rocafella Records in 1996. The first release on the label was Reasonable Doubts, Jay-Z's first album. They then released a movie, "The Streets is Watching," which grossed two million dollars. They then signed a deal with Deaf Jam in 1999 for a 33% stake in the label for 1.5 million dollars. The next year they rolled out Rocawear clothing, and in 18 months, the clothing line grossed 80 million dollars in revenue. It seemed that Jay-Z had the golden touch. After a list of platinum singles and albums, he became a star.

In 2005 he became Def Jams president. Jay-Z helped turn around the company. He signed a list of major acts that are still relevant today. Artists like Rick Ross, Jezzy, and Rihanna. That year he later opened a string of gentlemen/sport's bars called 40/40. He didn't stop there. He partnered up with Mikhail Prokhorov, a Russian billionaire, in 2004. This meeting would make Jay-Z part-owner of the Brooklyn Nets. He played a pivotal part in bringing the new Barclay's stadium to Brooklyn. Jay-Z could go on for days speaking of the many investments and deals he has had. He has had his own color, jeep, app, streaming service, movies, Broadway plays, restaurants, record labels, alcohol, etc. The list goes on and on.

After all these great accomplishments, Jay-Z wasn't done yet; his biggest and greatest move in my eyes was the re-construction of his own record label in 2008.

Jay-Z did a deal with the concert promotion company called Live Nation for a whopping 150 million dollars. With an extra 50 million dollars to start his own label. With that move, his life's dream Roc Nation was born. Jay-Z has excelled at so many things that it is hard to talk about just one. Just to say he is a rapper would be a grave misinterpretation. The fact that Jay-Z sold drugs as a musician, clothing designer, film, and NBA team owner would be an understatement. He had to hustle! He had to grind to make it where he wanted to be in life. That shows a lot about his character. When he got rich, he still never stopped! He said a little prayer and kept playing the game by staying focused on becoming a successful businessman. So, I ask you and myself, would we respect Jay-Z or look at him the same if he just was a platinum rapper. That is the joy of his manifestation because no matter what people thought, he didn't see himself as just a rapper. He saw himself as a capitalist that was born into this capitalist America. Fighting a systematic system designed for him and you and me to fail. Jay-Z learned how to capitalize off everything that he touched, anything that he could grab, he hustled. He excelled, evolved, and hustled everything to make a dollar off of it. Jay-Z did this while staying focused and letting his greatness manifest. He got the touchdown, and then he kept going. Jay-Z wasn't satisfied with rap; he stayed grinding. Simply put, not spiking the ball; he just kept winning.

CONCLUSION - I read this book once called in the shadow of saint death by Michael Delbert. In that book, it was a passage that caught my eye. "The HSBC money-laundering included such hard to detect gambits as a drug dealer walking into HSBC'S Mexican branch and depositing hundreds of thousands of dollars in cash at a single time, as this was going on, during the bailout of the US financial system that began in 2008. Bank of America received 45 billion while Wells Fargo received 25 billion of US taxpayers' money."

"At the time of writing this book, the United States had the highest rate of incarceration in the world and despite more than half of American Federal inmates being in prison for drug-related offenses. No one ever went to jail for the bank's role in facilitating bloody cartel business. It was an irony not lost on the bankers themselves. The bank and the senior bankers feed of money, money is the business of the bankers and the drug dealers produce a lot of money. A former official with the US bank with extensive experience tracking and analyzing money laundering schemes told me, "Yet the marriage is disturbed and imbalanced in favor of the banker."

"Nowhere can this be seen more clearly than in the criminal justice system and the prisons, which are full of drug dealers and void of money laundering bankers; one of the supreme ironic and twist is in the US system is the bankers using drug dealers money, to loan to securities companies to build more prisons, into which he drug dealers will be incarcerated for long periods of their lives. So, you are paying to house yourself. WOW!"

In conclusion, I pray that this book defers kids, young adults, and anyone with the will to change from going down a path of crime. Again, I want to stress that beware if you choose the streets! There will be times when you are broke, in jail, prison, and lost in this world! Getting robbed, shot, and all kinds of bullshit. This is just the bad side of the game; it's not all balling, hoes, cars, jewels, and big houses. So, prepare for the obstacles. In life, if you choose that route, I pray you don't go down that path.

With that being said, let me drop this last jewel on you. This is strict to all my street people; sometimes in life, on your path to greatness, people get blinded by what is really behind your grind, your motivation for success. The reasons that you would give your life and all your worldly possessions to save that person from harm's way, but that's natural even a bird watches over their family. So as a man, you should be proud that you want nothing more than to provide, protect, and love your family. So as a street nigga I can tell you that the street life will make you lose that reason and vision. You will be motivated by the wrong things and ultimately slip. So, to all my street people, stay focused on the goals and vision you started with and mainly stay sucker-free, and I promise it will happen. However, we have to change the way we play the game.

I wrote this book to try and save you from the pain and destruction. On this side of the game, to tell you that I wouldn't refer this life to anyone I loved. I want everyone who reads this to challenge themselves to be real, be better humans, and have better morals and goals. There should be a million laws that a man lives by, but I've only given you fourteen out of my life. So, your job is to build on my laws, learn from my mistakes and moves, and make your own to have a better life.

There are always twists and turns in these laws and in the game of life. Remember that in the game of power, the main rule is there are no concrete rules simply because life itself is so unpredictable. So, the best solution for that is to think unpredictably, yet have predictable standards, morals, and rules, then carry them out systematically. The great Hue Heffner once said. *"I am a rebel a man out to work hard and play hard to ,because you only get one time around in this old world and if you don't make the most of it then you got nobody to blame but yourself."* Trust your instincts above all. Be true to yourself and the truth will spread to the people around you. Always remember that a real hustler finds ways to get paid by the path of least resistance, so think before you go down that path and never play a rigged game. Thank you as the reader for going down this journey with me. I pray that we both end life on the right side of this road.

ABOUT THE AUTHOR

Pachino Allen Williams was born in 1979 in Atlanta, Georgia, where he was an excellent student but was swayed by the street life. At an early age, he started a life of crime. Pachino would work his way up to a high level of drug distribution by working for the Mexican Cartel. He made millions of dollars and started a record label that produced a hit record and received multiple awards and street accolades. He owned clubs and restaurants in Historic Downtown Atlanta, a barbershop in Thomasville, Georgia, a car wash in Moultrie, Georgia, and a host of other investments in companies that he helped get off the ground.

In 2010, he went to prison for a murder he committed in self-defense while getting robbed. Upon his release, he started multiple community organizations, private companies, and businesses to help the community. He fought his way inside the prison system to be a better man and, ultimately, outside in the free world to help his people. He is a real hustler and survivor. and all-around "go-getter." Through his obstacles and roadblocks, he made it from the streets to Wall Street. He preserved in prison, where he wrote this book to ultimately reveal the Art of the Hustler!

REFERENCES

Chapter (1)

1. "There is no such thing as bad publicity except your own obituary." **(Brendan Behan)**

2. "Never change for the mainstream--stay in your lane, and if you're talented and resilient enough the mainstream will come to you." **(Russell Simmons)**

3. "Understand: you are one of a kind. Your character traits are a chemical mix that will never be repeated in history. There are ideas unique to you, a specific rhythm and perspectives that are your strengths, not your weaknesses. You must not be afraid of your uniqueness, and you must care less what people think of you." **(Robert Greene)**

4. "Your only real fear should be that one day you will start to listen to what other people say about you." **(Philipp Meyer)**

5. "We think that what matters in the work world is gaining attention and making friends. And these misconceptions and naïve are brutally exposed in the light of the real world." **(Robert Greene)**

6. "It is a general rule of human nature that people despise those who treat them well, and look up to those who make no concessions." **(Thucydides)**

7. "It does take courage to grow up and become who you really are." **(E. E. Cummings)**

8. "As an egotist of the strong variety, you trumpet your individuality and take great pride in your accomplishments. If others cannot accept that or judge you as arrogant, that is their problem, not yours." **(Robert Greene)**

9. "A weak person goes where he is smiled at." **(Zulu African Proverb)**

10. "I am the owner of my might, and I am so when I know myself as unique." **(Max Stirner)**

11. "If you are dependent on their judgment for sense of worth, then your ego will always be weak and fragile; you will have no center or sense of balance. You will wilt under circumstances and soar too high with any praise. Their opinions are merely helping you shape your work, not your self-image if you make mistakes; if the public judges you negatively, you have an unshakable inner core that can accept such judgment, but you remain convinced of your own worth." **(Robert Greene)**

12. "If you have no confidence in yourself, you are twice defeated in the race of life with confidence you have won even before you have started." **(Marcus Masiah Garvey)**

Chapter (2)

1. "Habit is either the best of servants or the worse of masters." **(Nathanael Emmons)**

2. "No one was born wise." **(Ptahhotep)**

3. "Knowledge is power." **(Sir Francis Bacon)**

4. "To know ten thousand things, master one the others are worthless first it will become your habit then your nature." **(Miyamoto Musashi)**

5. "There are all kinds of rules that govern behavior values of good and bad, power networks that must be respected, patterns to be followed for successful action. If you don't patiently observe and learn them well, you will make all kinds of mistakes without knowing why or how." **(Robert Greene)**

6. "Value learning over money." **(Robert Greene)**

7. "Understand! The real secret, the real formula for power in this world, lies in accepting the ugly reality that learning requires a process, and this, in turn, demands patience and the ability to endure drug work." **(Robert Greene)**

8. "If you are unsure of a course of action, do not attempt it; your thoughts and hesitations will infect your execution timidity are dangerous. It's better to enter with boldness, and any mistakes you commit through audacity are easily connected with more audacity. Everyone admires the bold no one honors the timid." **(Robert Greene)**

9. "People who cling to their delusions find it difficult, if not impossible, to learn anything worth learning, a people under the necessity of creating themselves must examine everything and soak up learning the way the root of a tree soaks up water." **(James Baldwin)**

10. "Know the other, know yourself, and victory will not be at risk knowing the ground. The natural conditions and victory will be total." **(Sun Tsu)**

11. "To master any process, you must learn through trial and error your experiment, you take some hard blows, and you see what works and doesn't work in real-time. You expose yourself and your work to public scrutiny; your failures are embedded in your nervous system: you do not want to repeat them; your successes are tied to immediate experiences and teach you more." **(Robert Greene)**

Chapter (3)

1. "Tallyrand's ability to suppress himself in conversation to make others talk endlessly about themselves and inadvertently reveal their intentions and tactics were like no one else; he fired a pistol into the air to see who will jump out the window." **(Napolean Bonaparte)**

2. "What you do not reveal to people is all the more eloquent and powerful." **(Robert Greene)**

3. "Oysters open completely when the moon is full; and when the crab sees one, it throws a piece of stone or seaweed into it and the oyster cannot close again, so it serves the crab for meat. Such is the fate of him who opens his mouth too much and thereby puts himself at the mercy of the listener." **(Leonardo da Vinci)**

4. "Never interrupt your enemy when he is making a mistake." **(John Milton)**

5. "All of man's troubles come from not knowing how to sit still alone in a room." **(Blaise Pascal)**

6. "When deeds speak, words are meaningless." **(Mali African Proverb)**

7. "The capacity to see the reality behind the appearance is not a function of education or cleverness. People can be full of knowledge and crammed with information but have no real sense of what is going on around them." **(Robert Greene)**

8. "While spies give you a third eye, disinformation puts out one of their eyes a cyclops will always miss his target." **(Winston Churchhill)**

9. "Before it is too late, we must wake up and realize that real power and success can come only through mastering a process which in turn, depends on a foundation of discipline that we are constantly keeping sharp." **(Robert Greene)**

10. "It took this period of forced isolation and repetitive labor to transform him into a genius." **(Robert Greene)**

Chapter (4)

1. "There are individuals who would rather perish than work without taking pleasure in their work." **(Fredrick Nietsche)**

2. "There can be no progress or achievement in life without sacrifice, and a man's worldly success will be by the measure that he sacrifices." **(James Allen)**

3. "The competitive dynamic of the streets and the business world is, in fact, the same, but apparently, a comfortable environment makes it harder for you to see it." **(Robert Greene)**

4. "Everything turns gray when I don't have one mark on the horizon life seems empty and depressing I cannot understand honest men they lead depressing lives full of boredom." **(Count Victor Lusting)**

5. "Hustle- is staying ahead of your karma." **(Phillip Meyer)**

6. "You must act as if it is impossible to fail." **(Zulu African Proverb)**

7. "The only thing standing between you and your goals is the bullshit story you keep telling yourself as why you cannot achieve it." **(Jordan Belfort).** ''**The Wolf of Wall Street.**''

8. "Never stop your progress for more power return to square one psychologically rather than growing fat and lazy with prosperity." **(Robert Greene)**

9. "Most of the important things in the world have been accomplished by people who had kept on trying when there seemed to be no hope at all." **(Dale Carnegie)**

10. "America is a capitalist country and I am a capitalist." **(Alanzo**

Herndon)

11. A proverb says, ''All hard work begins a profit, but mere talk leads to poverty.'' **(Proverbs - The Bible)**

12. "There is in this world no such force as a force of a man determined to rise." **(W.E.B. Du Bois)**

13. "Only the weak rest on their morals and not on past triumphs in the game of power; there is never time to rest." **(Robert Greene)**

Chapter (5)

1. "He who has slacked his thirst immediately turns his back on the well, no longer needing it." **(Balthasar Gracin)**

2. "Do not imagine that your master's dependence on you will make him love you. He may resent you and fear you; it is better to be feared than loved; fear you can control love never; it is changeable fear will not." **(Niccolò Machiavelli)**

3. "Reality has his own power, you can turn your back on it, but it will find you in the end and your inability to cope with it will be your ruin." **(Robert Greene)**

4. "Any enemy who does not respect you will grow bold and boldness makes even the smallest animal dangerous." **(Robert Greene)**

5. "The key to life is always be willing to walk away." **(Frank Lucas)**

6. "People who praise you too much or who become overly friendly in the first stages of knowing you are often envious and are getting closer to hurt you." **(Robert Greene)**

7. "There is little friendship in this world and least of all between equals." **(Sir Francis Bacon)**

8. "Beware of feedback from friends whose judgments could be tainted by feelings of envy or the need to flatter." **(Robert Greene)**

9. "Be polite, be professional but have a plan to kill everybody you meet. In other words, make friends out of potential enemies." **(General James Maddy Mathis)**

10. "Abraham Lincoln's choices were pure pragmaticism; he was a keen observer of human nature and stuck with Ulysses S. Grant because he was the only General capable of effective action; he judged people by results, not friendliness or political views." **(Robert Greene)**

11. "The sense of having doubters or enemies can serve as a powerful motivating device and fill you with added creative energy and focus." **(Robert Greene)**

12. "If you go looking for a friend, you are going to find them very scarce if you go out to be a friend, you'll find them everywhere." **(Zig Ziegler)**

Chapter (6)

1. "Masquerade as a swine to kill a Tiger the easier it is for him to think he can prey on you; it is far easier for you to prey on him." **(Chinese Proverb)**

2. "The hunter does not lay the same trap for a wolf as for a fox; he does not set bait where no one will take it; he knows his prey thoroughly its habits and hide always and hunts accordingly." **(Robert Greene)**

3. "It's not the strongest of the species that survives nor the most intelligent but the one most responsive to change." **(Charles Darwin)**

4. "Nobody can give you freedom, nobody can give you equality or justice or anything if you are a man, you take it." **(Malcolm X)**

5. "If your part of the battlefield is covered with thorns, you do not leave or position and go to stand where the ground is so good." (**African Proverb**)

6. "It has always been a rule that the weak should be subject to the strong and besides: We consider that we are worthy of our power." (**Athens Representative to Sparta**)

Chapter (7)

1. "It's not the strongest species that survives nor the most intelligent but the one most responsive to change." (**Charles Darwin**)

2. "To have ultimate victory, you must be ruthless." (**Napoleon Bonaparte**)

3. "Diversification is a protection against ignorance diversification is not required if a person knows where they are going." (**Warren Buffet**)

4. "Focus on whatever venture offers the most realistic opportunity to make the most money." (**Jay-Z**)

5. "Dream big be unrealistic." (**Jay-Z**)

6. "Should you find yourself in a chronically leaking boat, energy devoted to changing vessels is less likely to be more productive than energy devoted to patching the leaks." (**Warren Buffet**)

7. "If you fail, how would you know how to succeed." (**Bobby Williams - My father**)

8. "All that glitter is not gold." (**Miguel Decervntes**)

9. "Occasional mistakes are inevitable; the world is just too unpredictable. People of power, however, are undone not by the mistakes they make but by the way they deal with them." (**Robert Greene**)

Chapter (8)

1. "Goals are not absolutely necessary to motivate us; they are essential to keep us alive." **(Robert H. Schuller)**

2. "Every struggle, whether won or lost, strengthens us for the next to come; it is not good to have an easy life." **(Cheyenne Native American Tribe chief)**

3. "Prince's and republics should content themselves with victory, for when they aim at more, they generally lose the use of insulting language toward the enemy arises from the insolence of victory or from the false hope of victory which later misleads men as often in their action as in their words for when the false hope takes possession of the mind it makes men go beyond the mark and causes them to sacrifice a certain good for and uncertain better." **(Niccolò Machiavelli)**

4. "Necessity is what impels men to take action and once necessity is gone, only rot and decay are left." **(Niccolò Machiavelli)**

5. "Live with your head in the lion's mouth-life is war." **(Ralph Ellison)**

6. "The moment of victory is often the moment of great peril in the heat of victory; arrogance and overconfidence can push you past the goal you had aimed for and by going too far, you make more enemies than you defeat do not allow success to go to your head there is no substitute for strategy set a goal and go for it." **(Allan Greene)**

7. "Know your enemy." **(Ron Casanova)**

Chapter (9)

1. "A philosopher and scientist in the 19th Century compared life to a chess game and said, "If it was so, we should at least consider to learn the moves and pieces. **(Thomas Huxley)**

2. "Space we can recover time never." **(Napoleon Bonaparte)**

3. "Hide your moves discretely place your iron hands inside a velvet glove." **(Napoleon Bonaparte)**

4. "Being emotional in business slows down money; keep a clear head it enables you to think of ways to make money or ways to stop you from losing money." **(Bobby Williams - My father)**

5. "To gain much, you have to sacrifice much." **(Napoleon Bonaparte)**

6. "The great oak is born out of the acorn." **(Allan Greene)**

7. "Business is the art of extracting money from another man's wallet without resorting to violence." **(Max Amsterdam)**

8. "Book smarts can be gained, common sense is not at all that common in people and street smarts ain't cheap smart it might cost you your life." **(Bobby Williams - My father)**

Chapter (10)

1. "You can't control a large group of people on your own you will either turn into a micromanager or dictator, making yourself exhausted or hated; you need to develop a team of lieutenants who are infused with your ideas, spirit and values." **(50 Cent)**

2. "Influence, on the other hand, is not power; it is the attempt to alter another more powerful individual or group opinion or action to your advantage." **(Amos N. Wilson)**

3. "The best way to find yourself is to lose yourself in the service of others." **(Gandhi)**

4. "We are all human and we have our positive and negative factors; those who look for perfection in humans are going to become demoralized, frustrated and unable to function, not realizing that perfection does not exist in themselves." **(Robert Greene)**

5. "If a hoe is out of pocket nine times out of ten, it's because of his poor ass pimpin in the game they say a hoe is a reflection of her pimp so the pimp has to set the proper example to get proper results if you are a lazy ass pimp who doesn't want shit don't be surprised when you have some lazy ass hoe's around if you look like a bum and don't care about your appearance or hygiene then your how's will most likely follow suit."
(Pimpin Ken)

6. "Avoid the unlucky the reason is simple humans are extremely susceptible to the moods, emotions and even the way of thinking of those whom they spend their time with." **(Robert Greene)**

7. "Nothing pains some people more than having to think." **(Martin Luther King)**

8. "We like those who resemble us and are engaged in the same pursuit; we like those who desire the same thing as we do." **(Aristotle)**

9. "Just as a gardener weeds out all the wrong in his garden, you have to weed out all the useless and impure thoughts and cultivate toward perfection." **(James Allen)**

10. "Never forget that even when your employees share your passion and your vision, they still have to eat, their primary motivation is going to be money that's just human nature; that's why you should never hold back financial incentives for them even if it cuts into your own profits for yourself it never lasts." **(Russell Simmons)**

11. "Studies show that many people stop pursuing a goal not because they are unwilling or unable to put forth the effort, but when they put forth the effort, the goal as promised is not there." **(Robert Greene)**

12. "Power is the ability to define reality and make others accept your definition as their own." **(Wade W. Nobles)**

Chapter (11)

1. "A sovereign should never launch an army out of anger; a leader should never start a war out of wrath." **(Sun Tzu)**

2. "Emotions lose money if you stay calm and cool; you then can figure out either a solution to save money or make more money; when you get mad, you don't think." **(Bobby Williams - My father)**

3. "Every struggle where won or lost strengthens us for the next to come it is not good for people to have and an easy life they become weak." **(Larry D. Crawford)**

4. "Birds flying against the wind are the strongest those flying with it are the weakest." **(Alan Greene)**

5. "True courage is knowing how to suffer." **(Haitian Proverb)**

6. "It is said that one cannot teach or bring another person to a level past that which he/she has reached him/herself." **(Warfield Coppack)**

7. "To show your frustration is to show that you have lost your power to shape events; it is helpless an action of a child who results to hysterical fits to get their way; the powerful never reveal this kind of weakness." **(Robert Greene)**

8. "Never show that something has affected you are offended; that only shows you have acknowledged the problem contempt is a dish that is best served cold and with affection." **(Robert Greene)**

Chapter (12)

1. "He will find that as he alters his thoughts towards things and other people, things and other people will adhere towards you." **(James Allen)**

2. "Blow yourself up like a building demolition; instead of tearing it down blow it up completely to rebuild a new." **(Jeff Johnson)**

3. "The shortest and best way to make your fortune is to let people see clearly that it is in your best interest to promote them." **(Robert Greene)**

4. "To succeed in the game of power, you have to master your emotions, but if you succeed in gaining self-control, you can never control the temperamental disposition of those around you and this presents a great danger most people operate in a whirlpool of emotions constantly reacting churning up squabbles and conflicts." **(Robert Greene)**

5. "You must change your style and your way of speaking to suit each person." **(Robert Greene)**

6. "The dictionary is the only place where success comes before work." **(Vince Lombardi)**

7. "Surround yourself with people who are going to lift you higher." **(Oprah Winfrey)**

8. "The men who have changed the universe have never gotten there by working on leaders but rather by moving the masses; working on leaders is the method of intrigue and only leads to secondary results working on the masses, however, is a stroke of genius that changes the face of the world." **(Napoleon Bonaparte)**

9. "Ironically, things that cost us money can be replaced; a good man or woman can experience bankruptcy but live to build another fortune that can be done several times; even if a home burns down, it can be rebuilt, but the things we get for nothing can ever be replaced." **(Robert Greene)**

10. "The best way to boycott is to build your own." **(Chuck D)**

Chapter (13)

1. "Our ancestors were kings and queens in Africa; that's why we love the gold and diamonds and flashy things; it's because we're supposed to have it we are royalty." **(Pimp C. UGK)**

2. "Build real commitments to diversify in your organization just because they look different or dress different doesn't mean they are different." **(Russell Simmons)**

3. "Money other can attain: power as well, but superior intelligence, good looks, charm- these are qualities no one can acquire, so they envy you for them." **(Robert Greene)**

4. "The people are always impressed by superficial appearances of things the (Prince) should at fitting times of the year keep the people occupied and distracted with festivities and spectacles." **(Niccolò Machiavelli)**

5. "A man needs to conquer women actually reveals a tremendous helplessness that has made suckers out of them for thousands of years look at the part of a person that is most visible their greed, lust, their intense fear these emotions they cannot conceal and which they have the least control and what people cannot control you can control for them." **(Robert Greene)**

Chapter (14)

1. "Man is made or unmade by himself in the armory of thoughts he forges the weapons by which he destroys himself or builds himself." **(Sigmond Fraud)**

2. "This past, the negro past of rope's, fire, torture, death and humiliation, fear by day and night fear as deep as the marrow of the bone this past this endless struggle to achieve and reveal and confirm a human identity yet contains for all in harbors something very beautiful people who cannot suffer can never grow up can never discover who they are." **(James Baldwin)**

3. "If one continually survives the worst that life can bring, one eventually ceases to be controlled by fear of what life can bring." **(James Baldwin)**

4. "Human nature is so constituted that it cannot honor a helpless man, although it can pity him, and even this it cannot for long if the signs of power do not arise." **(Frederick Douglas)**

5. "Stand on your own two Black feet and fight like hell for your place in the world." **(Marcus Garvey)**

6. "There is no cure that does not cost." **(Zulu - African Proverb)**

7. "We all grow up with the weight of history on us our ancestors dwell in the attics of our brains as they do in the spiraling chains of knowledge hidden in every cell of our bodies." **(Shirley Abbott)**

8. "Whatever the mind of a man can conceive and believe it, he then can achieve it." **(James Allen)**

9. "A man cannot ride your back unless it is bent; keep standing tall keep climbing." **(Martin Luther King)**

10. "The greatest weapon in the hands of the oppressor is the mind of the oppressed." **(Steve Biko)**

11. "We have conveniently forgotten that the land we now stand on was once the possession of the indigenous people who are now disproportionately concentrated on the reservation and reduced to alcoholism." **(Mwalimuk Baruti)**

12. "There is nothing more dangerous and destructive in a household than a frustrated, oppressed Black man." (**Nathan McCall**)

13. "The negro must remake his past in order to make his future."
(**Arthur A. Schaumburg**)

14. "Racism systematically verifies itself anytime the slaves can only
be free by imitating his master." (**Jamal Abdullah Al-Amin**)

15. "I've freed thousands of slaves. I could have freed a thousand more
if only they knew they were slaves." (**Harriet Tubman**)

16. "The blood that unites us is thicker than the waters that divide us."
(**Randell Robertson**)

17. "At a minimum, nearly three hundred million Africans were
murdered in that part of the mafia that is more than this country's
population today; the wrongful death of five to six million European Jews
at the hands of their brothers does not compare with king Leopold's
massacre of ten million Congolese Africans." (**Mawalimuk Baruti**)

18. "Poor is the apprentice that does not surpass his master."
(**Leonardo da Vinci**)

REFERENCES

1. "THE NEW JIM CROW" Michelle Alexander

1. " BLACK PROPHETIC FIRE" Dr. Cornell West

2. "UNFINISHED NATION" Alan Brinkley

3. "SLAVERY BY ANOTHER NAME" Douglas A. Blackmon

4. "BEFORE THE MAYFLOWER" Lerone Bennet Jr.

5. "ASAFO" Mwalimu K. Bomani Baruti

6. "DESTRUCTION OF BLACK CIVILIZATION" Chancellor Williams

7. "MALCOLM X" Alex Haley

8. "DARKWATER" W.E.B. Du Bois

9. "AFRICAN FUNDUMENTALISM" Marcus Garvey

10. "EMANCIPATION FROM MENTAL SLAVERY" Marcus Garvey

11. "THE MAKING OF A SLAVE" Willie Lynch

12. "THEY CAME BEFORE COLUMBUS" Ivan Van Sertima

13. "THE AMERICAN SLAVE COAST" Ned & Constance Sublette

14. " BLACK INDIANS" William Loren Katz

15. "FROM BABYLON TO TIMBUKTU" Rudolph R Windsor

16. "THE HISTORY OF THE NEGRO CHURCH" Carter G. Wilson

www.ingramcontent.com/pod-product-compliance
Lightning Source LLC
Chambersburg PA
CBHW070917120626
46546CB00001B/300